ISBN 3-936226-03-02

Published by:
Excalibur Editions
Heidemarie de Melo
Schleissheimerstr. 220
D 80797 Munich
Germany
Tel. +(49) 89 30 34 81
Fax. +(49) 89 30 80 646
E-mail: de.Melo.Horus@t-online.de

Printed in Germany.
First edition, October 2003
Cover design by Remko Arentz: 'The Sun'
With special thanks to NASA for imagery.
Title in German: Jenseits der Angst, ISBN 3-936226-02-04

ACKNOWLEDGEMENTS

I would very much like to acknowledge the following people. These people have supported this work and without their love this book would probably still be just an idea.

To my partner Remko Arentz for you love, support and continuos cups of tea!

To Peter White, for being a true friend to me and the animal kingdom. Your dedication to animal welfare is well celebrated amongst foxes and deer!

To Stuart Wilson, you have been a blessing in my life! I sincerely thank you for all your hard work with the preparation of this book.

To Heidemarie de Melo for your belief in my work – I could not have dreamed of a better publisher, thank you my dear friend.

And finally to the Ascended Masters El Morya and Sananda. It has been a great joy to bring through this work.. Words cannot convey the love that I feel in my heart for you, I cannot thank you enough.

INTRODUCTION

What follows is a dialogue that took place nine years ago between the Ascended Masters and myself. Most of the dialogue took place in my cosy little cottage in Devon. However, it wasn't just limited to the confines of my home. At times I would be walking my lovely dog Floyd and have a familiar spinning feeling. This spinning feeling is like suddenly going dizzy and I would have to stop walking and hold onto something – usually a tree – to steady myself. A 'voice' would then speak to me very loudly and I was convinced anyone within a short distance of me must have heard it too! I was often surprised when people would say that they hadn't heard a thing, but they could feel a dramatic energy change. Usually I had been thinking or contemplating on something and they would come in and answer my thoughts. It was as if my thoughts were not my own, were no longer private, they would know exactly what I was thinking at all times! A great deal of these communications were done whilst I drove my car. I remember pulling up at traffic lights chatting away to my unseen friends and someone in the car alongside staring at me, probably wondering who I was talking to. Even the bath wasn't sacred. El Morya has a very loud voice and would interrupt my thoughts to tell me to check my motives. I would often feel as if I was being pushed further than I could go, and I would cry and stamp my feet in protest at their demands on me. These demands were to help me to master every aspect of self, which I found to be often painful and challenging. Of course I realise now that they could only press those 'buttons' in me that were there to be pressed! As soon as I had learnt and mastered certain things in my life those buttons disappeared.

Throughout this book I have tried to involve you the reader as much as possible. Hopefully adding my thoughts and feelings throughout brings in a sense of participation.

I do not believe that it takes any great abilities or any special psychic gifts to be in communication with these beloved souls. I certainly never had any abilities in this direction as a child, and I had a very normal everyday kind of childhood. My parents are not religious at all, and they are very sceptical about 'Spirit'. *'Scepticism is just fear,'* Sananda (Jesus) once told me. '*Discernment is the ability to choose having first heard without fear'*.

This book has the title 'Beyond Fear' for only when we go beyond fear can we be free of our limitations, only then can we truly walk amongst the Masters.

INTRODUCTION FROM THE MASTERS

I asked the Masters if they would like to say a few words about this book.

Here is their message:

'Welcome, we greet you in love. We are honoured to be a part of this work. Although not large in size, it is packed with wisdom. For we have a message to deliver. Our messages are always short and sweet. We never use words for the sake of making our message longer, just to fill an empty space on your page. To do so would contradict that which we have come to teach. Many like lengthy messages with detailed information, do you not know that this only adds to your confusion? And so we say only that which needs to be said for we do not waste energy.

'This book comes at a very important time, for your world is undergoing a big transformation. These changes will send many into fear. It is therefore important that all learn to move beyond fear and into a place of complete trust. This place of trust is the final resting ground for the personality.

When the personality lies down – there rises the Master!

So Be It'.

ABOUT ME

Another page turns, and so comes the end of a chapter, the end of a very beautiful and special chapter in my life. This chapter has been about nine years in all, and although my 'book of life' is not over, not complete as yet, I am filled with cherished memories of that which has been, and filled with wonder at the next chapter that awaits me.

First let me set the scene. I have moved home now, a different environment than that where it all began for me - the sleepy coastal village. I now live on Dartmoor where the energy is quite different. The countryside is very 'moody'- the weather can change in an instant, thick mysterious mist can form a blanket over you, suddenly blocking your view, and forcing a quick retreat back into the warmth of our bungalow.

I live with my partner Remko, a gifted musician, and my old faithful pooch Floyd. We live quite simple lives, nothing fancy, and yet I am filled with a sense of peace which I know does not come from an external source. I feel that the reason for my peace is because I have finally found myself! I know and understand myself to the point where I can feel at peace. It has been a lengthy process and although at times I still find myself being thrown off balance by life's challenges, on the whole I feel very content. I trust in life now. I know that there is always a bigger picture, even if we cannot always see one. God knows exactly what 'He' is doing – all the time, and in that I trust. Knowing this can bring a sense of relief and peace into one's life, when everyone around is panicking and worried about life's events and dramas. Knowing that God is in complete control can help put things into perspective, and definitely helps to take the pressure off.

I understand now that peace also comes from living my own truth. This book is my truth. I offer it to you with the intention of passing on the wisdom of the Masters, so you too can find that peace within your own life. Let's begin!

CHAPTER 1

AN OPEN HOUSE

'In my Father's mansion there are many rooms, some do not have the lights turned on, but ALL rooms are still part of the same mansion.'

As summer faded into Autumn and the dark evenings began to draw in, I would sit in front of the crackling fire in my cosy cottage and await my next teaching. These teachings would come almost continuously, and it seemed as if I was being pushed to absorb as much of their wisdom as I could. And so began that evening's teachings in the usual fashion. First the room would be prepared, It was as if the atmosphere in the room changed. It became very soft and dream-like, almost sparkling with golden energy. Then one of the Masters would speak in a clear and direct way, and to me it seemed as if the voice filled the whole room.

This evening it was Sananda who spoke. I would sit and engage him in conversation late into the night and sometimes into the early hours of the next morning. At the time I was asking him how I was to find 'my truth'- how do I find my path, the path that would lead me home? He had advised me many times to 'live my truth' but I asked him, 'If you don't know what your truth is, how do you find it to live it?' This was his answer:

'Firstly, you need to unravel some of these many layers that you have encased yourself in since you first began to physically incarnate on planet Earth. This is a planet where you learn by experiencing everything physically. During the first incarnation when you began to experience something physically, you interpreted it, and put it into a category, i.e. pleasure, pain, suffering. In doing this, you built a false belief which put a layer around you. You did so to protect yourself. Then you had another physical experience and again you judged it as being either good or bad and another layer was built up. You met many people along the way, including your family, and they were all were doing the same thing, so you also learned from them and added layers to yourself that were not even your experiences! But you put them around you anyway, just in case you needed protecting! You then had another life and again, came and experienced, and a few more layers were added. You met more people, had another family to look up to, and again more and more 'protection' went around you.

'Now, think how many lifetimes you have had here! How many people you met along the way, each with their own experiences and judgements. Is it any wonder that mass consciousness believes in pain, sickness and suffering? You have encased yourselves in so many false beliefs that you have forgotten who you are. You have built up far more than the opinions of one lifetime. You have ended up looking like an Egyptian mummy with so many layers around you. Begin to peel off the layers that encase you and re-discover who you are. Begin to let go of all that is not you.'

I found it interesting to see that we create all these patterns in our lives without even realising it. We sabotage ourselves, and most of the time it isn't even really our issues – we just make them our own! Sananda said that we are to learn what is us and what isn't. For example, I was speaking to a friend one day, and she invited me out. I can't remember what the event was, or where we were to go to, but I remember that it wasn't something that I would normally do. My instant reaction was "No, I can't do that!" I then realised what had just happened, and said to myself 'Hang on a minute, that's not me! That's my mother speaking!

She is the one who is too polite and frightened to experience anything new. That's not me!' I then freed myself to be able to say 'yes' to my friend, and we had a lovely time!

Sananda said:

'To understand what is you in your unlimitedness and what is you in social consciousness (which is limiting) is the key. Before you act or react to anyone or any situation, it is wise always to try and find where the response came from. If it is not from your unlimited self then change it. Take the unlimited option, for only in this decision lies growth'

He continued:

'Do not do only that which feels safe, try exploring all of Gods creation, do something that you are scared to do, move beyond your comfort zone. We will walk with you, for we shall honour your courage.'

And so I quickly realised that this path takes guts! It is not for the faint hearted! We all have skeletons in out cupboards – things about our lives and ourselves which we would prefer to keep hidden but Sananda said that to be a Master requires us to have no skeletons. It is my belief that the higher the vibration on the planet the quicker that which is not 'your truth' will be stripped away, leaving only that which is you - the real you! So how do we tell what is truly us?

'When you are living your truth you know it! You begin to move into that magical river where life flows, for the Universe is with you – or rather you are flowing with the Universe. When this occurs the Universe turns its full attention to you and all of its energy, abundance and joy are yours. This is how to create peace in your life – flow with the Universe.'

And so I made the commitment to begin to 'find myself.' I decided I didn't want to be encased in illusions and wished only what was truly me to remain. The Masters had told me that it might not be easy, for very few had ever lived on the Earth and truly been themselves – what a strange thought! I decided that I didn't want to be my mother or my father, my sister, friend or cousin from a previous lifetime – I wanted to be *me*. And so I set out on a quest to find myself. Nine years on I feel that I have moved a little closer to that goal that I then set myself .

I was told that mass consciousness is vast and filled with negative thought patterns that have built up since life on Earth began. This will take some time to release. The best way to help clean up mass consciousness is by working on ourselves.

I sat and contemplated on their words. I found that to contemplate what I was told helped me to integrate the information fully and make it my own. Without this process, they would just have remained meaningless words.

I began to think about negativity and protection and wondered what Sananda's views on this subject might be. After all what are we protecting ourselves from? I knew that all there is 'out there' is energy and this energy is what is called 'God' or 'Source'. So why protect myself from God? I was puzzled. I had been told by others that we have to protect ourselves from all of those 'negative' entities that are waiting to grab us and devour us the minute we let down our guard. Well, I was told that our Light is the only protection we will ever need. If our love is strong enough it will conquer all, or maybe conquer is the wrong word here. Let us say when love meets an energy that energy has the chance to become love too, thus returning to wholeness. I know that a great many people are scared and fearful of the dark and other entities and so I questioned Sananda further. He gave me this beautiful analogy about fear, dark and light which I would like to share with you:

' In my Father's mansion there are many rooms, some do not have the lights turned on, but ALL rooms are still part of the same mansion. A Master is one who can walk from room to room without judgement. He / she is not afraid to enter into a room and see what lies within for he/ she knows that every room is part of the whole and therefore part of God. If you want to be as the Master, then keep on walking, don't become attached to any one room, even one that is light, for this too is a trap – perhaps the biggest trap! Many in the 'new age' movement have fallen for this trap, and they are being encased in more and more layers of illusion, for they are building themselves another false identity.'

Wow! This was somewhat of a shock to me. I always thought that those in the new age movement had a special dispensation - that perhaps we are the 'advanced ones'! How wrong I was! I asked him what he meant by this, about the new age movement and illusions.

'There are some who have locked themselves away from society as a whole – locked themselves in a lit room as it were. It is fictitious to assume that we are closer to you, and that you are closer to God when you are only doing that which fills you with love and joy (the lit room) We are with you at all times. To stay in a 'lit room' is like only firing on two cylinders instead of six! It is true to say that I shall wait at the doorway, until you are ready to come out and look at the whole you! I do not need to come into the lit room with you. I know you are already in there, it is filled with your illusions about yourself and the world. Come with me into your darkness, there we shall uncover the real you!

'Now, this also can be a trap! Do not stay in the dark room either. A Master walks from room to room, never staying in one room too long, never becoming attached to any one room. Your world is filled with dramas, each room is filled, in their own way, with tempting offers to stay longer than need be. Now temptation comes in many forms - you are not always tempted by the gold!

I shall wait outside the door until you seek to know yourself. Eventually you shall dwell neither in the light nor the dark but in perfect balance, you will have befriended you whole self.'

Sananda said that it can be very tempting to stay in that which is light (the lit room) He said that if it was true that we should ignore our dark side then he would never have come to Earth to begin with – he would have stayed in the light having harps played to him all day. (He has a good sense of humour!)

I asked him to explain more about 'dark energies' and what should we do when we come across someone 'very dark' and negative. If we are not to protect ourselves against them and 'close down' what do we do? He replied that there is no need to do anything! There is not the need to judge them as being 'dark' or 'negative'. He said that to love them increased our Light which, as said before, is the only protection we need. He said to love a person doesn't mean that you have to agree with them or like what they've done or are doing. Look to the soul of the person and love that, not necessarily the 'little personality' running around on the Earth plane! He said that to protect ourselves continuously is fearful and this is defeating the object of becoming Light! To become Light means to have no fear, for fear is darkness.

'Light vibrates at a different frequency, the higher the frequency the more Light you can carry. Somebody or something that you would call 'negative' has a low frequency, a low level of

Light- as it were. However, they are still Light! They could not be alive without Light! Many focus too much on the dark in others and in situations, we ask you to see the Light in order to increase the Light. That which you focus your attention on becomes reality – this is creation!

Expanding on this topic a little further, I then asked him about different religions, cults, and groups and what he thought about those who say that their way is the only way, and that everyone else is wrong, misguided and even deceived into believing something different. He said:

'It is a very shallow river that does not allow water from many parts to flow in.'

He went on to explain that when he lived on Earth as Jesus he would travel to many places, listen to everyone and judge none. He said if we are firm in our truth and living it, then there is no need to judge another for their truth. He said that he loved people so much and that he found everyone so interesting that he would take into himself everything everyone taught. The reason that he was able to do so was that he had no fear. Because of his love he was able to let everything in – keep nothing – and just allow everything to pass through him. That is the way to keep expanding, by being an empty vessel. He told me that he didn't need protection for he loves ALL of life. Still on the subject of protection, I asked him about someone verbally attacking us. What do we do? Do we 'turn the other cheek' and try to ignore it? He said :

'Do nothing!'

He said what we shouldn't do was to go into 'defence mode' and defend our point of view or actions. He said we should listen to what the person had to say and take it to our hearts - perhaps they've got a point! But we have to be very honest with ourselves: it's very easy to defend ourselves by thinking that, 'That's all their stuff.'

'If you search your soul and still find nothing then you simply say to the person that you don't have a problem, and that if they do, then that's their problem!'

He said we are scared to be defence-less because it makes us vulnerable. He asked that we try and be defence-less for he can reach us then, not when we are 'holding it all together!' To be vulnerable is not a weakness but an asset for we become as children – innocent and ready to learn. We then went on to the subject of healing, I asked him if there was anything that I could do to help the planet.

' There is a big illusion. Many feel the need to try and fix everything, sort and heal everything. There are many groups around the world who are stuck in a 'glamour' room, they travel around various places doing various rituals and sacred acts to heal the land. Why do you feel that you need to fix anything? Unless you have specifically been asked by a 'messenger' to do something, then don't do it, for you could be interfering and doing more harm than good. It is ego that wants to join in with ceremonies and it is ego that wants to make a difference. You will know if you need to do something specific, you will get a 'push' or a visitation.

'Likewise if someone wants your help with healing or guidance they will ask for it, do not impose healing upon them, even absent healing. If you really want to help, then first acknowledge all is as it should be. A Master focuses on the perfection, not the imperfect.

All that you should do is to heal yourselves, be the healed healer rather than the wounded one. Become Light by carrying more Light in your aura, thus everyone coming in contact with you will subtly begin to raise their own vibration, and their consciousness will raise. To be an example is all that is necessary, you do not need to say a word!'

This can be difficult, for we often feel the need to 'talk our truth' to others. Because we cannot see our Light and its effects, we do not feel we are doing anything worthwhile. Sananda told me that the more we raise our own vibration, the more we become Light. The more Light that we become, the more mass consciousness will begin to change – subtly. We shouldn't get into the glamour and the trap of thinking that we are here to 'save the world'.

Late that evening, in fact it was three in the morning, he awoke me to discuss emotions! I can tell you that I was pretty 'emotional' at the time about being awakened at such an hour – couldn't it wait?

'In this world of polarity, you live within a complex array of emotions. It is true to say , however, that there are only two

emotions, love and fear. All other emotions are 'off-shoots' of these. You are to learn from your emotions, and then master them. Do not deny that they exist, and do not wallow in them either, but look at them and learn from them. Only then can you find the 'middle way'. Don't be afraid to know your WHOLE self and do not just look at those parts of self that feel safe. It's like saying, "Well I will go here, but I won't go there. If I totally ignore my dark side, and act as if it never existed in the first place then maybe it will go away". Why not love your dark side as well as your Light? After all, it is still part of the same 'mansion' . This is a big issue which causes one of the biggest separations there is. It causes judgement.'

> *'Understand that everything that is alive is love.*
>
> *There is nothing that is not alive.*
>
> *Everything is alive, therefore everything is love.'*

Throughout the year and a half that I spent 'in training', a lot of that time was spent in tears! Although Sananda and El Morya were very loving and supportive throughout this period, they were also firm. They certainly were not going to support my illusions, my false self that I had created. And so layer by layer they helped me to chip away my false ego. There was many a time when I would get angry, stamp my feet and shout at them, and they would always answer in a way that was constructive, never pampering or endorsing my ego. Once I said to El Morya, 'El Morya, you're so strict!' and he answered,

'I am not strict, I am just more focused than you!'

CHAPTER 2

WISDOM THROUGH EXPERIENCE

'Wisdom comes through experience: don't deny yourself experience, for you deny yourself wisdom.'

Many times the Masters would 'arrive' rather inconveniently when I was in the bath! I learnt to keep a writing pad and pen with me beside the bath just in case one of them had something to say!

On this particular day it was Master El Morya who came to teach me about the subject of wisdom. He told me that these are key words:

'Wisdom comes through experience: don't deny yourself experience, for you deny yourself wisdom. Whenever you go into fear about something, and that fear stops you from experiencing, you are denying yourself wisdom. Truth is only yours if you really experience it for yourself.'

I now understand why I was kept from attending other people's workshops. It wasn't a judgement on them, it was just that they were teaching *their* truth and I couldn't make it mine. I would have to experience what they taught first before I could gain the wisdom from it. Yes, I could maybe find it of interest, and it might give me more insight, but if I had gone to find my truth, I would have found someone else's truth. And then maybe I would never have found it within myself.

There was a time when some of my friends were going to a talk given by a lady who is well known and respected by many in the new age movement. Even though the Masters had said I was not to go to this talk, I really wanted to! And so I decided, 'No I wanted to go, and too bad if the Masters didn't want me to!' I didn't understand their reasons, and so I decided to go against their advice and go anyway! I got ready and sneaked out of the house, thinking that they wouldn't even notice that I had gone! I tried to start the car, and guess what - yes, you've guessed it – it wouldn't start! Well, as you can imagine, I was pretty cross, and felt a little silly at the same time, thinking that I could outwit the Masters! And so I demanded an explanation!

'We advised you not to go because you are at a vulnerable stage in your own development. If you were to attend this talk you might hear things that contradicted what we have been teaching you. Because she is well respected and well known you would begin to doubt yourself, and us. Understand that we are not saying that what she is teaching is wrong, it is just coming from a different approach, a different angle as it were. She is a beloved soul, and what she teaches is valuable to those on a similar path, and remember all paths lead home eventually.'

And so I learned to trust the Masters. Even though my ego became angry with them from time to time, they were always patient – firm, but patient. I also felt some conflict within me when I was asked to *'Just be'*, for I felt that this was in conflict with what they had told me about *'Experiencing life to the full!'* He replied :

'To 'just be' you may argue is not experiencing much, but we say to you that when you do that you start observing life, and this is the richest of experiences. Watch nature, look at the sky, observe other people who are probably going about their business of 'doing' – take it all in! Running around the countryside, in search of

yourself, you actually run further from yourself! When you take the time to stop, slow down, you allow yourself to catch up! You probably will feel a sense of conflict, for the generation that you have grown up in has taught that to 'do nothing' is lazy, and that to 'get anywhere in life' means to push forward, work hard for what you want, is this not true?

'We are telling you the opposite of what you have been taught since you were a child and so we realise that there will be conflict. When you stop and slow down you allow yourself to 'catch up'. You can then gain far more than you realise, for in that stillness lies your real power. We also understand that to' just be' can be a little daunting for some, for by doing so they shall experience themselves. When one is constantly in a state of 'doing', what you are really doing is avoiding yourself and your emotions. Many ones, we note, announce that they want to 'find themselves' – become whole again. Well, to do so requires that you 'just be' with yourself, and stop avoiding your emotions.'

A lot of this year was spent alone and in my cottage. Because of this I had a lot of time to 'go within' and learn about myself. I felt, however, that this wasn't experiencing much, but then I was quickly reminded that to experience all of life didn't necessarily mean 'doing'. We often avoid going within – into inward self-study, and would much prefer to bury ourselves in the rush and hubbub of life. We would probably rather find some form of entertainment to amuse ourselves, for isn't this what life is all about? Having fun, living life to the full?

'No, this is not what life is all about, this is avoidance. It would be preferable at this time for you to retreat for a while from 'entertainment'. This is not to say that you are to abstain altogether from 'fun pursuits' as you call them. It is just to recognise when it is the time for self reflection, observation, inward study, and then spend the time going within.'

He continued:

'To live a life that is continuously wishing for fun is to seek a path that you can never fulfil. As soon as this fun is over you are in search of the next event. This is a form of addiction, being addicted to fun or happiness which is the emotion which is created through having fun. A Master is not addicted to his chemical responses. In other words a Master doesn't experience 'fun.'

I questioned this for at the time I thought 'How boring! I'm not sure if I want to be a Master, then!' He replied:

'When a being reaches a point where they have mastered their emotions they do not wish or crave for the thrill of 'fun and excitement'. They reach a new point of understanding which is called stillness within. This stillness is a calm and peacefulness that is quite blissful. Once this stillness has been acquired, I tell you now daughter, that you will never wish to go back to your 'fun and exciting life'. This will be meaningless to you. You will see it as glamour and as an illusion, for one is never truly happy having this fun, it is very 'short lived'! – and remember, I chose my words carefully!'

I can now vouch for this. At the time I found it hard not going out, for I had had many years of wild parties, pubs, clubs, boozing, drugs and other forms of illusions! However, I can now say that I reached a point, a turning point in my life, where I found that stillness is peaceful and blissful. It changed me as a person, I no longer need fun and entertainment and am now content with life. The wisdom then, came from experiencing myself.

And so my life changed – totally, and with that change emerged a much stronger sense of self. I was having a discussion with El Morya about change, and how difficult we humans found change to be. Here is his view on the subject of change.

'One of the biggest fears for man is fear of change. Because of this fear you would rather stay as you are than 'risk' stretching out a little further. Out into the unknown. You have probably heard of the saying, 'Better the devil you know' (than the Light that you fear!)

'However, to become 'stuck' can lead to a hellish situation. The problem is that the longer that you 'live with the devil' the harder it becomes to pack your bags and walk out, (out of the dark room). Every time that you move a little further out of your comfort zone the more that you will grow, for wisdom will be gained through the experience. Big changes do not necessarily need to take place in our lives, at least not all in one go. Just take a small step forward each time, growing more and more confident, never pushing yourself too far as that will be an extreme action. Know that the Master walks the middle path, and , as we said, does not experience extremes. Although to find the middle path you have to know where the middle is, and that takes experience!'

I would say that most people who have fear in their lives have probably 'swung their pendulum' to one extreme and are too frightened of change. In a funny sort of way they feel comfortable and even safe. It can also feel like such a long way back to the middle path. I can understand this because I feel that I have allowed myself to experience extremes in my life. For example, I went into the drug scene quite young at the age of fifteen and experienced some pretty negative things over the years. As we know, when someone is hooked on anything they will do anything to get it, and love doesn't come into it at all. This can become a hellish situation, and the middle road can seem such a long way away that many do not know where to start their long journey home. Also they may find that they are pretty tired and weary through their experiences and can't be bothered to attempt this journey, and so will stay with 'the devil they know'. This staying put attitude, however, is missing the chance to gain much more wisdom through experiences. Experiences help us to grow, for we learn so much about ourselves. However, if your comfort zone has lost its appeal to you, then I would suggest change in some form is advisable. As the Masters have said, we can make the changes by just taking small steps, we do not need to 'dive into the deep end,' for this is an extreme action - better to start at the shallow end.'

I have noticed another kind of fear, and I feel this is very deep rooted. Many people suddenly discover what it is that they have to do here on Earth, what gift that they have to offer to the world. And as soon as they discover it they run from it! They've been searching for it all of their life and asking, 'What is it that I came to do?' And as soon as they know, they turn and run back into that safety zone once more. I feel the reason is that they are too scared to do what they came here to do in case they fail! The thought of failing is so great that it is better not even to try because the actual failure would be too great to take. The biggest excuse is, 'Well I don't feel that quite I'm ready yet'. Well, when will you be ready? When you are at your last breath? Too late! I argued with my teachers about this when I was asked to start giving talks and passing on the Masters' wisdom.

They said:

'YOU ARE READY NOW! You are the perfect person to do the job, you already have all that you need to begin the work, you came in with it. You have had the appropriate training throughout your life. You have the knowledge and the wisdom that is

necessary. If you did not know what it was that you came to do, then you would probably still be in the process of unravelling the many layers of protection and illusions that you had placed around yourself. You cannot truly know yourself until you let go of your 'armour'.'

Do not allow fear to stand in the way of achieving your earthly goal. It really is better to at least give it a try than to have regrets later. Personally I feel that that would be a greater sense of failure. At least you could comfort yourself with the knowledge that you had tried, and in so doing you had gained a little wisdom!

'Let go and don't judge the outcome, and also don't have expectations of the outcome.'

The Masters told me that they have witnessed us going through the death experience many times only to 'kick ourselves' on the other side because we were too afraid to live life to the full. In our limited life we have evolved very slowly and continue to reincarnate until we can evolve past emotional attachments and fears.

'Have the experience but do not become 'bogged down' by the experience. Just experience it – in a detached way – witness the experience, do not judge it, just observe. This is the way to flow through the experience of life. If you allow the experiences in life to stick to you, you grow denser and heavier making it harder to move forward. To avoid any experience is fear. To 'sit in your cave' is avoidance and it is fear- based. Allow yourself to have a wide range of experiences but never hold onto them, even the good ones, let them flow through you, just let them come and go.

'Many ones fear and try to avoid what they would consider to be bad experiences, thus placing a judgement upon that experience. It is a life of illusion that wishes only to experience 'the good things in life'. As you have been told, it is like staying in a lit room, and that is the biggest trap there is!'

I asked a question that has been asked me many times before: 'What about experiences that we as human beings definitely would consider to be 'bad experiences'? Situations such as 'choosing' to experience famine in a third world country or fearful experiences such as those Jews must have faced throughout the second world war?' I was curious to hear what the Masters had to say on these subjects.

'You are asking a very third dimensional question and expecting a third dimensional reply. This answer lies outside of the third dimension.

'Understand that no soul is ever without control of their own life, even if from a third dimensional view point it may look that way. To do so would be to take away your power. You have complete power and are in complete control, you have free will to express yourselves as you wish. Remember that you do not always need to see the bigger picture in order to know that there is one. It just takes a little bit of faith and trust in God. God allows all souls to carry out all experiences. As we have already mentioned ALL experiences help you to gain wisdom, even those bad ones that you mentioned.

'Now, in a way it is a good question and I will make a third dimensional attempt to answer it. So, why would a soul chose to have such experiences?

'Imagine, if you will, that on a higher dimension you knew only Light, and that Light was so brilliant that you felt totally loved and whole. That wholeness was so peaceful and calm you didn't know

anything outside of it. It was clear to you that there was more to reality but you didn't truly know it, for you hadn't experienced it. Now let us suppose that this was a brave soul, and that that soul might say, "Well, I'll have a go at experiencing life on a physical planet, as a physical person, in a dense body. It can't be that hard! And while I'm at it, I'll see if I can make a difference to this world! If I'm going to do this then I might as well go into real density. Yes, put me in a situation that will really test my ability to be God.'

You see, that is what life on Earth is about, testing your God-like abilities, your Light, your strength, your power and will in quite difficult situations –if I may put it like this!

'To be God-like in denser conditions is not so easy! And so you see it is truly you who tests yourself. Of course when one travels down through those finer vibrations into dense matter it suddenly becomes apparent that perhaps this 'act in the play' might not be so easy after all! Especially when your memories are taken whilst coming down into matter. You literally are like a baby in a foreign land. This is why souls become trapped on the Earth plane, because they are blind as it were. They forget that they are God and quickly lose their power and their ability to be God. Therefore it can be a long and tiring journey back to the God-like state of being.

'To be God, is to know that you are already God. Try to understand that although you are now in dense physical matter and on a dense physical plane, this doesn't mean that you are by any means cut off from God. How can you be when you are God?

'You see, God isn't a being, as such, that sits on a throne in a far off place called Heaven. That belief is for those who wish to hand their power over to a religious structure. God is a Presence that is all-pervading. That means God's Presence is everywhere. For how could God be in one place but not in another? It is not possible. And so you see you are not alone, cut off from God. God's Presence is all around – experiencing life through you!'

CHAPTER 3

BEYOND DEATH

'The further you have progressed in Earth life the further you progress out of Earth life'.

Four years ago I had a 'near death experience'. At the time I had no idea just how close I was to dying. It was when I was recovering that the surgeon told me that I had only half an hour left to live when the ambulance arrived. So many people are frightened of dying that I thought it may be helpful if I shared my experiences. I also have asked the Masters about this subject in order to gain an understanding of the process.

In my first book 'Mirrors of Eternity' I tell my experience in detail. In this book I wish to begin from when I reached the hospital.

I was experiencing a terrific amount of pain, but this vanished as I was lifted out of my body. I am unsure where exactly I went to. All that I can remember is that it was very peaceful and beautiful. As soon as I left my body all of the fear that I had vanished, and I felt totally safe and loved. There were very gentle beings all around me, assisting me. These beings were not like anyone I'd ever seen before, and they were not human beings. They were silvery in colour with very large beautiful electric blue eyes. They had no nose or mouth, but they managed to communicate with me. This method of communication was through telepathy. They asked me if I wished to go with them or stay on this plane. Needless to say I chose to stay. This was certainly not a frightening experience, in fact it was very beautiful. The whole time I felt supported and loved. I asked the Masters to give some insight into death. Had I chosen to leave at that time what would I have experienced?

'The departure from the physical body would have been swift. This would have been due to the fact that you were not so attached to the physical form as many people are. The more trust that you have, the swifter the passing. Now let us at this point state very clearly that, of course, there is no 'death'. It is impossible to 'die', it is a transition. We are using the term 'death' simply for your understanding. The transition is meant to be a beautiful experience, it certainly was not meant to be something to fear. To be released from the physical body is a very freeing experience. The only reason that ones would experience difficulty in transit is

through fear and through attachments. One only has attachments due to ignorance. This may sound harsh, but if people were educated in the process of transition then they would understand that nothing is ever lost. Therefore if you know you could never lose something or someone, why would you ever want to be attached to it? It's this clinging on, this gripping tightly to someone or something that makes the process uncomfortable for some.

'Now let us explain the process. When you depart from the body, it is not that you are 'wrenched out' gasping for air as some fear! You do not need to breathe for you do not have lungs that need air. You 'slide' out of your body and effortlessly travel through a portal into a new dimension. Many have spoken about travelling through a tunnel when experiencing a 'near death' situation. This tunnel is a portal into another realm. You are met and aided either by relatives that have already 'died', or by guides, Masters or Angels depending upon your acceptance levels. You can only go to the dimension that you have evolved to. In other words, someone's life on Earth will determine where their life continues on another plane. You are unable to go to an 'advanced' level if you have not advanced much in your Earthly life. You would not be in harmony with it, your vibration would not match. And so you go to a vibration – a dimension – that you energetically match.

'Some lower levels are very 'Earth- like'. There are cars, houses, hospitals, shops and even work to do (as if you haven't done enough work already!) This plane of existence is created by those who resonate with this level. In other words they feel at home with objects, people, work, and Earth-type experiences and so they continue to experience them. The further you have progressed in Earth life the further you progress out of Earth life. These higher frequencies – higher dimensions – are exquisite. There are still some buildings, but they are built from geometric designs to enhance the energy flow. The buildings are mostly used for teaching and for healing purposes. There is a calmness, a sense of peace and tranquillity that is difficult to explain in words. The light here is different, soft and yet vibrant. There are very advanced realms where ones move beyond the need for form and become one with the 'Mind of God.' These are the co-creator levels. One would be suspended in a space of utter love and peace. Thought would have been mastered to a very high degree to be at one with this realm. All realms beyond the Earth plane are timeless. In other words you will not experience time.

'Throughout all levels of existence there are opportunities to advance onwards. There are schools of awareness to aid this advancement. The Earth plane has always been held in high

regard. It is understood that on Earth the rate of advancement is superior to any other realm. Having a physical body is considered to be a very small price to pay for this advancement, and so there is a large ' queue' waiting to re-enter this plane. Do not be in such a hurry to discard your physical bodies.

'There is a process that you go through that determines your available options. It is called a life review. This is what is often known as Judgement Day by religious people. This is when you re-experience your life, in other words your life is replayed. You experience the impact your life has had on others by feeling the emotions as it returns to you. For example, if you have been a kind, considerate and gentle person then you shall experience these qualities. Whereas if you have been unkind, hurtful and cruel then you would experience these emotions that you inflicted on others. What goes around comes around.

'During this 'review' you will also look at missed opportunities – or missed 'time-lines'. These 'time- lines' could be viewed as a corridor with doors along either side at certain points. The path – or corridor – that a person was walking along would have certain opportunities (doors.) If the person missed the opportunity, or didn't wish to take it (perhaps out of fear) then the person would remain on that same time-line. If, however, they chose to take the

opportunity and walk through the 'door' then they would be entering onto another path – or time-line. Some of these time lines are higher in vibration, some are lower, depending on the choice made. You will know in your body when you have taken a different path and entered onto another time-line for you will feel an energetic change in your body. This, as we have said, depends on the vibration of the time-line as to whether it is an uplifting feeling or one that is more dense.

'Now what we were endeavouring to tell you in the previous chapter, is that whenever you miss an opportunity, you will see all of these missed opportunities in your life review.'

I was fascinated by these 'time-lines' and asked the Masters to explain more about them. For example, how do we know if it's a high vibrational choice or a lower one? I felt this was important for me to understand as I wanted to take only the higher choices. Surely then, these higher choices must mean that they are for the highest good?

'If you are travelling along your path – a time-line – and there are many experiences that seem to be difficult, you may try and force change. This is called struggle. If you succeeded at 'forcing

open a door' you may well enter into a lower vibrational time-line. This of course would then alter your course, but not necessarily to the course with the most potential for your growth. Strangely enough the path that you were on, that you found to be difficult, could have contained the most potential for growth!

Now, it is most advisable to stay on the path that you are on until an opportunity presents itself to you. When it does, give it some thought before leaping in. Try to imagine what could occur if you took this route, then make your decision.

' Some people feel as though they have 'gone backwards'. This could be because they had either opted out of a choice, (choosing not to go through a door, and to stay instead where they are) or even because they had decided to take a lower and denser option. This opting out choice is usually made out of fear of progression. Now, a choice that is made to enter into a denser time line could possibly be made by the soul. This decision could be to touch upon certain already experienced events that took place before, that were not truly mastered then. A person may have skipped through the experience previously. The purpose of this returning is to gain a better understanding of the situation and so another event would then be set up so that the person could experience a similar situation again.

'People, you will notice, depart from your life due to the change of time-lines. You may meet up again at a later time when another door is opened. Never judge a person who goes out of your life whether permanently or briefly, even if you feel they are on the wrong path, for there is no 'wrong path'. There is no 'highest good' as such, they are simply brave enough to re-enter into a denser time-line to return briefly to some experience. If they succeed in bringing Light into the experience this time then they will progress greatly.

'So highest good' then simply means allowing opportunities to be presented, instead of forced. If there was such a thing as 'highest good' in absolute terms then that would mean that there has to be a 'lowest choice'. This would then mean that there is a God who judges all experiences. You are the only judge of your experiences. You make the judgement based upon your emotional response. And so, when you experience your life review you will see all potential lines. You will see the lines that you missed and the lines that you chose to take.'

I was persistent! I wanted to know about someone who took a 'door' that led them to murder someone. Surely that could be considered a 'wrong' path?

'Understand that paths are not destined to be a certain way. Therefore there is no fated path or predestined path. All paths have the opportunity for growth. In a sense all paths could be considered to be 'empty' and yet filled with all potential.

'Now if we can briefly return to the information that we shared with you about a person whose path is filled with struggle, and because of that struggle that person wanted to move out of that path as quickly as they could. Now that struggle was self -created, everything you find along your path – you have created. Most of the time it is done unconsciously, but some of the time there is intent. Therefore if a person was to take a path that led him to murder someone, it would have been that person's state of mind that would lead him to this act. The 'path' would not be responsible, therefore you can now see that there cannot be a 'bad' path, it is what you create in the path that is important.'

CHAPTER 4

THE MASTER IN THE MIRROR

'Everyone in your life is a mirror, a reflection of some part of you. It is important to see and understand this in order to grow from the experience.'

Autumn turned into Winter and the roads became deserted as everyone in the village seemed to retreat into the warmth of their homes. My little cottage was warm and snug, although at times I would physically shake, and my teeth would chatter. Not from the cold, but from the intense energies that would build up. Looking out the window across a grey wintry landscape it felt as if everything had gone into hibernation. My cottage was very much alive: I often wondered what the neighbours would say if only they knew what was going on. I settled down to another day of teachings and the Masters announced that it was now time to start going deeper within, deep into my subconscious and face myself.

The Masters told me *'Do not look outside of self'*. This was one of the biggest points that they made. I was told that if I remembered nothing else of their teachings to remember this one point : '*Always return to self*'. Often we put things onto others so as to avoid looking at issues within ourselves. We know that life is a mirror of our own creations, we set the scene and we select the characters - or actors to play in the scene. We must remember that all of the actors are professionals! They are playing their roles perfectly. We draw the experiences and the people into our lives in order to create our own drama, and manifest our own reality.

'Everyone in your life is a mirror, a reflection of some part of you It is important to see and understand this in order to grow from the experience. It's easy to go into denial and think, "Oh, that person can't possibly reflect a part of me!", but I'm telling you, they ARE a reflection. It takes honesty with yourself, to see it. Do not go into defence mode either, defending yourself. Be open to the fact and see and learn about yourself.'

I reflected on this and noticed that some of my friends were powerful people and were fully embracing their power. They are confident, something I was not. My reflection was to embrace my own power and learn to be confident.

'If someone in your life is annoying you in some way, look to yourself . What you will find is that you are annoyed at a part of yourself. Others can only annoy you if you have buttons to be pushed! For example a person can be irritating because they interrupt you all the time or speak loudly and over the top of you. Perhaps this could be showing you that you need to speak out in some way, and quite possibly, if you are honest with yourself, you will find that you do the same to others. Perhaps someone is pushing your buttons by always being kind and nice. Maybe this shows that you need to be a little kinder to others and to yourself. If you are surrounded by kind considerate and caring people then it is reflecting your kindness. If, however, you have a lot of angry people around you, then it would be wise to address your own anger buried somewhere deep within you.'

I was told to contemplate long and hard and with absolute honesty until I saw the mirror. I was taught that our life is a reflection of how we think: our surroundings, our jobs, our friends, our relationships and our health. There is no getting away with the fact that we create everything in our lives, for whatever reason, we create it.

'If the life that you live is full of limitations and fear it would be advisable to look at why you wish to accept this reality. I wish to point out here that as the creators of your own reality you are fully responsible for your creations. Therefore it is no good blaming anyone else for your lives, whether in the physical or elsewhere.'

There was a time when I would try and 'hand over' to the Masters to solve my problems. One day they said to me:

'Stop handing everything over to us - we tell you now that we will not accept this responsibility. We refuse to take your power. We wish you to take back your power not continuously give it away! Even God doesn't want you to hand over anything to 'Him'. 'He' wants you to BE God. Re-claim your power by accepting that you are in charge of your own life.'

They continued:

'Many ones blame 'fate' for 'karma' for the way their lives are. In an act of defeat they look to the skies and say "This is the way it must be for me." This is not power, nor is it being a Master. To be

the Master requires that you start acting like one! Learn to take full responsibility for your life and take charge of it, not giving your power away at the first opportunity – this is a 'cop out' . If you do not like how your life is then it is you who must change it. Do not struggle to make changes in your life, flow and allow the Universe to present opportunities to you. It is then your job to choose what opportunity you want. Remember, the Universe will only give you those opportunities which are in alignment with your thoughts. The higher the frequency of the thoughts - the better the opportunities.'

I was told that I needed to understand energy and how we create our reality through our thoughts. I was also told that I needed to understand what Karma really was so that I need not fear it.

'Firstly understand that you create your reality, therefore if you wish to believe in Karma in your life, then So Be It! – It Shall Be So! Karma is your own thoughts that travel out and are held in your Auric field. These thoughts vibrate at a certain frequency. Energy comes along and those vibrational frequencies that match will magnetically be drawn to yours. So in that way you draw to you that which you put out. There is not a wrathful God who says,

"You've done this or that in this or some other life- time, so you must pay for it now!" This would be a judgement and God doesn't judge. And so you can monitor if your thoughts are positive and enlightening by the energy they draw to you. So with this understanding you now know that you cannot blame God, Spirit, the Universe or even us for that which enters into your life – you created it!'

I feel sad when I hear people say that they must have been bad in a previous life to have the experiences that they do in this life. I do not know about any other life- times that I have had. The Masters have always told me that it is important to stay in the Now and that it doesn't matter who I was or what I have done hundreds of years ago! What is important is who I am NOW. We need to claim back our power fully, not give it away to some fantasy or illusion about who we may or may not have been. We are to take full responsibility for who we are now, and what we are creating for ourselves. To do so we need to 'return to self' as I have been reminded many times before!

And so we draw our fears to us through vibration. Anything we fear we put energy into. That energy goes also into our Auric field and is held, stored there, vibrating away quietly to itself on a certain frequency! If we put a lot of energy into that fear enough energy particles will magnetically attract, manifesting that which we fear into our life. Likewise, that which we wish to create in our lives, if we put enough energy into it, it will be attracted into our lives, for like attracts like!

'And so, remember that there is no one or no thing out there doing something to you! You drew it to you for some reason. Quite often experiences in your lives reflect back your self love and self worth, how you consciously or subconsciously feel about yourselves.'

In a reading I was giving someone, the Masters talked a little about self worth. These are their thoughts on the subject.

'You all have choices in life. You all decide what seeds you wish to 'plant in your garden'.

'You are all the gardener. It is up to you whether you allow weeds to grow and overtake your flowers, destroying the beauty and peace in your lives. When someone knocks your confidence, you allow them to plant a seed of doubt in your garden. Perhaps

someone else comes by and throws in another, then another, until your entire garden is overtaken by strong and healthy weeds. Those weeds have suffocated and killed off your beautiful flowers that you first planted. Exhausted you sit and stare at the overgrown garden. You ask "Where do I begin? How long will it take to clear?" It seems a long road back to the beauty of a tranquil garden. Many ones will not even bother to try.

'Now, if we examine this little metaphor, every time you allow someone to knock your confidence and plant a seed of doubt, the flowers that they kill are your dreams. As soon as you let the first weed grow, others are quick to follow, as your confidence and self worth drops more and more until your garden becomes overgrown with other peoples thoughts and opinions. (Which as we have just learned, is probably only their opinion about themselves!) Now, when your confidence is low it is difficult to stand up and say, "Enough is enough!" and begin your weeding process.

'To begin to take control of your life once more requires that you choose to be the gardener once more! Look at what you have allowed to grow in your garden. Are people supportive, kind and loving to you? If not then why do you allow them to continue to grow in your garden? Probably because they began planting their seed in your garden such a long time ago that the spreading of the

weeds occurred very slowly over time and you never even noticed it happening until it was too late and you became entangled in the illusion. Begin to remove them one by one, do not allow anything less than love to grow in your garden. If you do this your self worth and confidence will return. You may find, incidentally, that you will be left with very few people in your life, but why would you wish for so many 'suffocating weeds' in your life anyway? Isn't it better to uproot the lies and re-start, or re-seed your garden again? The end result will be worth the effort, for the more love you attract to you, the more loving people will enter your life.

'For some, they have begun the 'weeding' process, and ask many times, "When will it come to an end?" Well, sometimes it is difficult to see just how much weeding has been accomplished when you are stood in the middle of your garden, surrounded by it all! Quite often you miss the beauty that you have begun to plant and focus only on that which you want to achieve. This is all right, as long as in doing so, you do not let more 'negative' seeds grow in frustration. This is why we say to you always to try and see everything from a higher perspective for then you will see things as they truly are. You will see that you are in charge of your own garden, and you decide what grows there. Time to take charge once more of your garden, let go of the 'weeds' that suffocate and

drag you down. Wouldn't it be nice to rest in a warm and sunny garden filled with love and peace? Well, it is possible! All that is required is for you to stand up, take an active role in your own life, and let love grow!'

CHAPTER 5

LETTING GO

'When you have let go of all that no longer serves you, you move into a new space, a new way of being. You live in the NOW.'

This chapter came about because I was having a difficult time letting go of certain issues. Although these times were very precious to me, they were also very difficult. Not only did I have frequent feelings of 'Am I going mad?' but I would also have people consulting me to get the Masters' advice about issues in their own lives. This would cause me some discomfort, as at times the advice the Masters gave would be challenging and I would worry about 'misguiding' anyone!

The teachings that follow in this chapter are about emotional attachments and how to let them go.

'To master your emotions you must learn to become emotionally detached. This means from ALL situations in life. That which you hold emotional attachment to becomes your greatest lesson.

'For example, the more emotional attachment that you might have to money – the less money you will have! The more emotional attachment that you have to an illness the worse that illness will become. If you had no emotional attachments, then nothing could effect you emotionally. Part of being the observer in life is not to hold onto anything or anyone. This does not mean that you will not have anything or anyone in your life, but to be detached means not to cling onto things or people with such an emotional grip.'

I was told that to master money issues I was to let go of it. (This was difficult to do at the time for I didn't have any spare to let go of!) I was told to let go in a balanced way, which means letting go of a small proportion of my income – even if only pennies – regularly. This would free up the emotional attachment which was causing the lack.

'If you hold emotion strongly in one direction you will create an imbalance and create a worse situation for yourself. You also need to be aware that if you are experiencing financial difficulties you may have to look at another possibility and that is that you are out of balance with your giving and receiving (second chakra). There should be a balance of energy going out from you in service equal

to that which you receive. If you are someone who is very giving, but does not receive much back, then be aware that this imbalance can cause serious imbalances in the body. Someone with this degree of imbalance may even end up 'giving away' an organ, a breast or having a hysterectomy. This is energy out of balance to an extreme.'

I have observed that when this is the case, the people concerned are very loving and give a lot of their time and energy to others. To correct the balance they would need to embark on a self love and appreciation process. This process would include boundaries – making clear boundaries and then sticking to them! Also, what is important for self love is receiving from others, perhaps a massage or a loving therapy. A massage is a wonderful way of receiving, and it also means having to let go and trust the person massaging you! Trust is usually also lacking in those who find it difficult to receive.

To have harmony in our lives means we have to find a balance in ALL areas of our life. If you can achieve this then you will not experience lack. Incidentally, you may say, 'I would love a massage, but cannot afford one!' Well, I was told that by having one anyway, you would actually start the process of freeing up abundance, for love starts flowing.

'Try to balance out your day.

'Find time to be alone, find time to be with others, find the time to do something creative and find time for the body. You can combine these together, for example, you could go for a walk, which is good for the body, and also go with a friend, which is your time spent with others. To find time to do something creative is very important.'

I was told that my soul was crying out to express my creativity fully in this life-time, and I believe this to be the case for all.

When I started out on the path to enlightenment I naively assumed that life would instantly be easy! All of my worries would disappear, abundance would pour through my door, I would have love and friendship from everyone around me. I would never be lonely or lost again! As I said – how naive! I assumed life would be easier and problems would be non-existent – not so. At least not to begin with. In fact, life becomes a great deal harder. It takes a real commitment to God, and this can be experienced as being very painful. The reason that it can feel this way is because when you commit yourself to God, life can never be the same again. Nine times out of ten, I would say, that life will become very crazy, anxious and an emotional rollercoaster for quite a number of years! It certainly is not a smooth and easy ride into the arms of God! Why is this? I would say that the main reason is because change will take place in your life, and sometimes big change. This depends on how much you have buried yourself into the three dimensional world and how much you have to let go of. I was told that when you commit to God you start to move away from structure, from work that serves only to pay the bills, but doesn't fully express who you truly are. At this point, the money one has often becomes less, and many ones seem to find themselves in a great deal of financial stress. As you begin to let go of emotional baggage, clearing out deeply buried patterns and hurts, often your health can deteriorate too. Friends who you've known and who have been in your life for years can suddenly depart, relationships and marriages can end. Many move house and all in all it can be a tremendously stressful, frightening and emotional time. Your self worth can take a battering.

'Now, the reason that these changes have to take place is because if you commit to God, you begin a purging process. To fully know and love yourself requires that you let go of all that is not you! And so you begin to purge out all that which is not really you. You cannot truly find you when it is buried behind material comforts. In other words, you cannot use money as a prop for your self worth. Where there is love there is life in abundance. So if you have a secure job earning lots of money but your job is not using all of your gifts and potential, your creativity, then it will depart, taking with it the material security. Life becomes far more than security traps and illusions. Now, your finances may well drop considerably whilst there is a re-shuffling, a re-organisation taking place, a shifting of your priorities. You often look at abundance to be in financial term: you have to move away from this concept and begin to learn to view abundance in different terms. You will more than likely find that your finances will stay less for a while, but your abundance in free creative enjoyable time will increase, making more time to pursue hobbies, and interests.

'Your health quite often fluctuates as you clear density but this is only temporary, it will eventually balance out and you will experience good health in abundance. Friends depart because you have to find the 'friend within' – in other words become your own

best friend. It is at that point that you will have an abundance of new friends. If you are in a loveless marriage then it will end. You will find it very difficult to remain anywhere or with anyone where love doesn't grow. Where there are any areas in your life that are based on convenience rather than love, a reshuffling will take place.'

I found myself thinking about the Tarot card 'the Tower' as false structure, with the ego and illusions crumbling away to reveal only the true self. And to make it sound even more daunting, I was told that this period can last many years, depending on how difficult we make it for ourselves. If we can easily flow with change then this time will pass by a good deal more smoothly. Personally, I haven't met anyone yet who can pass through all of these changes with ease and grace, simply because most of us have fear. It is frightening to let go of all our comforts, even when we know that we have outgrown them. It is difficult and hard to let go of the sources of our security, even when we know it is a false security. It is difficult and often painful to walk away from a marriage, a home and sometimes children. It is difficult to commit to the release of dense patterning within when we know that with the releasing process it will bring to the surface buried hurts and emotions. I asked ,'Why is it that many experience such difficulty in their physical bodies?'

'Your physical health will be weakened as you shake free of all your pasts.'

When we look at the road in front of us, we may well wonder why we would bother to make this effort!

'You bother because eventually, whether it be in this life-time or the next, sooner or later you will have to make the commitment. When you do so you release yourselves from the cycle of reincarnation. You bother because you know that all else is an illusion. The reason that it becomes painful and challenging is because you have allowed yourselves to become totally lost and absorbed in the illusion. You have had life-time after life-time to experience the illusion: perhaps sometimes you have briefly stopped and glanced down the road, but decided it was too scary to try just yet.'

The Masters continued:

'Now, there is *light at the end of the tunnel! Sometimes God can be like a hurricane that blows into your life, turning everything upside down, only to resettle it elsewhere. The light at the end of the tunnel then is the 'calm after the storm'. When all that is not really you – the real you – has departed. Like a tree stripped bare of its leaves after a storm. But afterwards, you become filled with a deeper understanding, a deeper sense of 'you. ' This deep sense of you will not leave, it will only increase from then on making your life enriched, not by material things, but enriched in the sense of spiritual nourishment. Your whole life will be nourished in ways that you could not have possibly imagined before. The life that you struggled to give up becomes meaningless, so you are glad to leave it behind because it is no longer such a big thing to do so! Once you have found God and allowed 'Him' into your life, then your life becomes very magical. You will not feel the need for anything , and you will be fulfilled and filled with a deep sense of peace.*

'Now life in general has a habit of trying to throw you off balance, but the peace – once found – never becomes lost, never again will you be enslaved - you cannot for you have already been freed. When you become emotionally detached then you cannot lose your peace within for you are the observer – as the detached traveller in this world you will not become trapped in it, in your

own illusions. The road never ends, it just keeps opening up, further and further, opening up to reveal another horizon. When you have a larger picture in front of you then you can remember how very limited your lives were before. As you step into your new horizon another one unfolds, only each one more enriched, more beautiful, more expanded than the one before.

'To truly know God is to know yourselves. You cannot truly know yourselves when you are encased in your illusions. The illusions must leave before you can find self. You cannot find self in the middle of chaos. It is like planting a rose bush amongst a lot of weeds and saying, "Now grow". You have to get rid of the chaos to allow your rose bush to expand, leaving it free to express itself fully in all of its glory!'

Well this was a very traumatic time for me, but finally I reached a point in my life where I felt very content, very much at peace with myself. With a sense of gratitude, I announced, 'At last I know who I am and what I am doing here!' The reply was a little unexpected!

'That's good - now let that go!'

I was confused and so I asked them to explain.

'To say that you know who you are and what your doing here is limiting, it is stopping you from becoming more than you are and it is stopping you from doing more than you can do! Don't limit yourself with these words and feelings, free yourself up to become more than you are now. Wherever you are in life you should be prepared to let go and move on.'

They told me that if, for example, we had been working with the same guides and in the same way for a certain length of time, we should be prepared to let them go too, so that they can grow onwards also.

A few years ago I worked with a Native American guide, by the name of Black Crow. He was wonderful to work with, his information and knowledge were incredible, and he helped me and others in so many ways. However, one day I had to let him go. He came to me to say 'Goodbye'. He said that it was now time for him to advance onwards and that I should let him go and learn to work with others on other levels. Although it was painful to let him go it was important that I did, as this opened me up to a long and wonderful period with the Ascended Masters. I was told that although it is very tempting and glamorous to stay working with the Masters it is also important that I become the Master myself. In order to do this I have to be prepared to let go of all levels, including the Ascended Master level in order to keep expanding.

I contemplated for a whole afternoon about letting go, and how do you know when you have really let go of something? I have tried the ceremonial burning of bits of paper with people's names etc on it, but it still didn't really feel inside that it had worked.

'You will know if you have let go of a person or situation – your past, because if you try to recall parts of it, it will feel as though it wasn't you, as if you were not even there.'

I know that I have let go of my childhood and am not dragging it along with me because if I try to think and feel back into my childhood it is difficult to really recall or recapture moments or events. It feels as if it wasn't really me, and for that reason I know that I have let go of it.

'The key is to have no emotional attachment to any time, person or place. To find out if you have let go of your past, try and recall a time and place. If you can say, "Yes, I can still vividly place myself there, and it is like I am still there. I can even feel how it felt at that time" - if this is your response then you have not let go.'

So how, I wondered, do you get to that point where you cannot really recall an event or have any feelings, because you have no emotions that are still connected to it. We know that events and people are just players, just actors that have played out a role to get us to where we are now, but knowing all of that isn't enough to let it go, particularly if it was a painful situation. So how do we get to that point? Well I was told that there is a certain procedure to go through.

'Firstly, you must be able to see yourself clearly in another time. As we have already said, this is the way to identify if you are still attached to that time. Once you have done so, the next step to take is to call your Spirit back, and you will probably feel the merging back of this part of you. The third step is to contemplate what is the key emotion that is attached to the situation.'

I had a little trouble with this, for I couldn't find my key emotion. The way that I found it was through giving the Masters an example of someone that I knew. I asked them if someone had been raped and left for dead, what would their key emotion be? Would it be fear? They said, '*No, fear is not an underlying emotion.*' After several minutes I finally realised that the underlying emotion for someone in this situation would be anger.

So having established this, I then asked what the next step was to release this, still using this as an example.

'To release anger, thus healing the past, would mean getting angry! In the case that we have just been studying, the person involved would need to get angry so as not to be a victim again. Now, be aware that this does not mean that she should become an 'angry person', that is something very different. She would have to wait until the 'healing opportunity' would present a chance to be angry.

'Now, there would have been many times after the event where Spirit would have provided her with opportunities to heal this. Probably, instead of becoming angry, she would have suppressed her emotions once more, thus reinforcing the victim mode.'

Now I could see how this could work, but I when I mentioned this to her, she wasn't happy about having to be angry at people. She asked me if this meant having to face the person who had done this to her.

This was their reply:

'No, we certainly are not suggesting that she goes on a quest to seek out her persecutor: this should be avoided, for we are not encouraging a 'witch hunt' here! What we are suggesting is that she should use the opportunity as it arises. Now, do not worry so much about the 'player' who has been 'signed up' for the role. Did you not know that sometimes a Master can manifest to give you an opportunity to do your healing?

'So if for example, someone gets angry at you in the street about something, instead of letting it go, get angry back, release the anger! You may even find that you turn around afterwards and they have vanished!

Now I had noticed a pattern in myself of always saying 'Sorry' for things, even if I hadn't done anything! If someone barged into me with their trolley in the supermarket it would be me saying

'Sorry'! It wasn't easy to find my underlying emotion, but I finally traced it back to feeling sorry for myself. In fact I realised that I was so sorry for myself that I had become a 'sorry person'! To heal this I had to stop apologising. As soon as I had realised my underlying emotion, a situation manifested to heal it.

It was that very afternoon, and as I sat in the office at work I had my handbag beside me on the floor. Someone walked past me and tripped over my bag – in fact they trod right on it! Automatically and without thinking I said 'Sorry' - and straight away realised what had occurred. The person then said, 'No it was my fault for being clumsy' . I just smiled and said, 'OK, apology accepted'.

Now to you this may sound rather silly, but normally I would have replied, 'Well I'm sorry, I shouldn't have left it there'. Just by responding differently released the pattern, it was as quick as that! Later on that same day I tried to see myself in the time frame that had sparked off the emotional response, but I couldn't! I wasn't there anymore! I had healed it, and it wasn't a long and lengthy process! I realise that my 'problem' may seem silly and unimportant compared with the example we looked at earlier - the rape incident For her to heal it may take several attempts to get angry, depending on how deep the hurt is buried and how much suppressed anger she still has. However, I have a feeling it might not take that long - my feeling is that healing can take place in a moment, you just need to change the pattern. The Masters told me:

'When you have let go of all that no longer serves you, you move into a new space, a new way of being. You live in the NOW. To live in the Now means that you do not have memory – for memory lives in the past. If you should ask us to recall a past life and give some details about it, we would not be able to do so, for we do not hold on to memory. Memory is dragging along a past. If we dragged along our past we would be unable to live in the Now, and it is in the Now that all of our power lives. And so we have let go of our past – as you too are learning to. This is why many of you are finding you are having difficulty remembering. We do not view it as a difficulty – more a blessing. By letting go of the memories which you cannot recall, you are learning to live in the Now!'

I was asked to give a talk about some of the Masters' teachings, but I was worried that I might not be able to actually remember their teachings clearly and so I asked them for their help with this.

'You are trying to recall something that you have integrated, therefore it is part of you now. You cannot recall our teachings as you would wish to, even if that would make you feel more secure, for our teachings do not belong to your past. This is why you have no memory of them as such. Go give your talk from the point of Now, and that is where you will find us!'

I questioned them further about this, and asked them about their other lives as I found it a little strange that they couldn't remember any details!

'To recall a lifetime means that we would have to re-enter briefly into that time frame and experience it again. This would be the only way that we could give you any details as we do not save the experience or store it up as a memory, for then we too would be dragging along our past!

'Understand then that when you have an experience – any experience – good or bad - it is important to let it go. Do not hang onto it. To hang onto a bad experience would only cause discomfort, judgement, grief, bad health and resentment. If you feel

any of these emotions, then you know that you have not let go of your past, you are still dragging it along.

'We notice that many of you do not like the feeling of being an 'empty vessel' – it feels unusual to be empty and uncluttered. So much so that you try to cling onto or grasp a memory - you think there is something wrong with you and worry that your 'mind is going!' Well it is in a positive sense! This could be the true sense of being 'brain washed!' It is a good sign that you are letting go of memory – which is your past!'

CHAPTER 6

HEALING BLOCKAGES

'Unlimitedness is where you will find us, for we do not reside in the limited mind.'

I have now let go of my past and have moved forward into the Now, so much so in fact that this next experience only took place a couple of hours ago!

I have noticed that recently there seems to be a reoccurring pattern that replays itself over and over. I get to a certain point in life, just when my dreams – my creations, are about to become reality and then they come to a complete standstill. I just couldn't understand why it was happening time after time. I knew I had to find the root of the problem for only then could I heal it, but what was the root? And how could I heal it? I knew that I create my reality – totally, and there was nothing out there apart from myself blocking me. But why was I blocking myself? I had been taught to create my reality consciously and I knew that when I *focused consciously* my creations *would* become reality. I also knew that the only reason that they wouldn't do so is because *I* was blocking it from happening. When I say consciously create, I mean through a focused visualisation technique I had learned. To do this simply means holding an image clearly in my mind for as long as I can. This image then creates because consciousness creates reality.

And so I set about releasing this blockage. I sat down with my eyes closed and repeated over and over, 'I am successful in all that I do'. I then felt a strange feeling in my throat chakra – a block! I kept repeating this until I knew I had gone through it. I realised I was still not getting to the root cause of the problem - I had successfully released something but not the root cause. I then tried going right into 'I am a failure' - I had to experience fully the feeling of failure before I could feel a success! And so I sat and repeated out loud 'I am a failure' over and over again I went into it quite deeply and experienced lots of faces staring at me and laughing. It was a horrible feeling, and I became tight around my throat again. I kept going until the point where I wasn't afraid of failure! It was strange as I sat with all of these people around me laughing and ridiculing me (which has happened on and off in this life) and all of a sudden I got to a point where it didn't matter anymore. What was failure and success anyway! It is only how we perceive something, a judgement we put onto an experience. I felt very empowered! It was at this point that I changed the wording to 'I am not afraid of success'. The laughing stopped, the people faded out into a bright golden light. I then saw a hand stretching out towards me carrying a silver platter and on it was a key. I had to use the key to unlock my throat chakra and as soon as it did a dove flew out of my throat!

I played around with words like this for a while and then discovered something that was hidden even deeper. I was afraid of my own power - does that sound familiar? Because I have been taught not to be afraid of 'entering a dark room' I decided to go right into being powerless, fully experiencing it so that I could come back out the other side of it. I repeated over and over again – about fifty times in all – 'I am afraid of my power'. I noticed a strange thing began to happen: I felt as if I was shrinking, becoming shrivelled up and dark in colour. I felt as if I was alone, isolated and almost how we could perceive the Devil to be! I started to feel tight in my throat chakra and began retching as if I was about to vomit. I knew I had reached right into the centre of the root cause. It was at this point that I began to reverse the procedure, re-patterning myself. I began to say, 'I am not afraid of my power'. Over and over I said it until I felt myself getting bigger and bigger, lighter and lighter, and the constriction around my throat disappeared. After repeating this for a while I changed it to 'I am a powerful being'. The power that I felt within me was amazing. Although I felt a little traumatised afterwards I realised that I couldn't really free the pattern without going fully into it until the point of not being afraid.

I tried the same technique on a friend who always said he felt cut off from the Masters and Angels and wished he could experience things as I do. After some time going through various affirmations he realised it stemmed back to feeling unworthy. The root lay in feeling cut off from God. He had to repeat 'I am worthy of being loved by God' over and over. After a while he broke down in tears and sobbed and sobbed. He now says that he feels totally connected and that changes have taken place in his thought processes. He feels re-connected and can now fully be an expression of his source.

For me, several hours on, I still feel a little traumatised, but I can feel dramatic energy changes throughout my body.

I realise that unless we can get to the root of the problem things will never change. We can go for readings, have infinite amounts of healing from others, sit doing burning rituals, affirm that we are this or that all day long, but it will never work. If you feel you have a blockage then you may like to try this method for yourself. To get to the root may take some time, depending on how deep the issue is buried within you, but persevere - it is worth it!

At this point I shall briefly explain a little bit about chakras. It is necessary to know about this as you are going to feel a reaction within one or more of your chakras when you are doing this exercise. It is therefore important to have some understanding of what each chakra relates to so that you can see the bigger picture and understanding more about the blockage.

The first chakra or base chakra relates to your foundations and security in life. Whenever your foundations are threatened you will become ungrounded. Often people who are moving home or changing careers can have a root chakra imbalance.

The second chakra represents giving and receiving and sexuality. A lot of health problems relate to blockages in this chakra as very often a person can be a giver but has trouble receiving gifts gracefully.

The third chakra is your willpower. If for example you suppress your willpower and become subservient then you will feel the block here.

The fourth chakra represents all kinds of support by the Universe - universal love, abundance etc. You will probably have a blockage here if you have issues relating to unworthiness.

The fifth chakra represents communication and all forms of expression.

The sixth could perhaps represent eyesight problems and headaches may well be related to this chakra, although I feel these problems may also come under 'health', so you may well feel a reaction in your second chakra as well as your sixth. The sixth chakra is also associated with inner vision.

The seventh or crown chakra focuses the incoming Light, and so it is related to truly becoming God on Earth. When you address your issues and blockages then you can fully express your Godself in the physical body.

Having briefly covered the chakras we can now put this information to practical use. Sit somewhere where you will not be disturbed for some time. Close your eyes. Begin to state an affirmation out loud without pause. Perhaps if you are unwell you could state, 'I am worthy of perfect health'. Repeat this over and over again until you feel some sensation in your body. Keep going, taking note of the chakra where you feel the sensation. Allow yourself to enter right into the feeling. If you want to cry – cry. When you reach this point you know that you are at the root of the blockage, so you can then begin to reprogram yourself with excellent health. Keep going with the affirmation until you feel a change taking place and the feeling goes from the chakra. You then know that you have healed the blockage and have reprogrammed yourself.

Energetically what happens is that when you get to the root of the problem you are entering into the time frame when it first took seed. You can only reprogram yourself if you enter into that time frame and change the seed pattern. It is important to realise that you do not need to see anything or re-experience the situation as in a regression. I am quite visual now so I was able to see certain images, but it is not necessary. By trying to see you will be taking the focus away from feeling. It is *feeling* that is important here because it is the deeply rooted feeling that makes you *feel* unworthy or unwell or unloved etc. When you emerge from the other side of the experience, you will notice that energetic changes are taking place so make sure that you nurture yourself for the rest of the day. You will then be able to continue the next day with your creating through focused visualisation knowing that you have cleared the blockage.

I asked the Masters to explain to me just how powerful and just how effective this technique really is.

'This technique is very crucial to all those trying to reach a certain level of self mastery. This is part of self mastery – to see clearly where you have a blockage and then use this ancient technique to release it. By doing this you will be writing a new script for yourself.

'It is difficult to truly move into areas of creating consciously when you have old dense patterns stored within. However, it is sometimes even difficult to know that there are issues to begin with, particularly if they have been stored over a length of time. These could well be so deeply buried and hidden that it is advisable for all to 'play around' with affirmations. By doing so you may be surprised at just how many different unresolved issues you still have!'

I was also advised that it is a good idea to return to the same affirmation a little while later just to check that I hadn't recreated the same issues again. I was told that we can easily do this, for if we have had the issue ingrained within us for so long, it can be hard to give it up!

'Now, blocks can come in many disguises. It is always wise to check - when you receive guidance make sure that it doesn't come from the 'saboteur'. In other words, make sure your guidance will benefit you, not sabotage your dreams and creations.'

I know this may sound a little bizarre, but they told me that we easily sabotage ourselves through fear, and many people carry a secret saboteur hidden deep within them. They said that they watch us doing so every day, and if the 'saboteur' has been hidden for many years it may have become invisible to us.

'When you are given choices in life it is always best to weigh up all the options and seek guidance from the highest level that you can. Do not always take the obvious choice.'

I was told to 'track the route' and see if a 'saboteur' was at the end of the trail!

'For example, it is wise to think carefully before saying 'No' to something for you may be sabotaging yourself through fear. If you

question yourself and discover that fear is the reason for you opting out, then it is advisable to reconsider. Doing that which is fearful may well be the best choice you ever made, for it may open up many doors which would otherwise have remained closed.'

So we are advised not to block ourselves from further adventures and to work on releasing our inner blocks to free up the 'outer' blocks.

'When you do so, many great changes can take place in your life, for you have entered into unknown territory. That unknown territory is called 'unlimitedness'! This unlimitedness is where you will find us, for we do not reside in the limited mind. There is another name for this unknown territory - it is also known as 'the void'. The void is where all potential exists – it's a good place to be!'

Many people are frightened by the idea of the void, but it is really very positive. Nothing is excluded from it, and so within it, all things are possible. Many artistic people are able to increase their creativity by embracing the void, because it contains every conceivable creative solution.

CHAPTER 7

LOVE IN ACTION

'Where there is compassion – Love follows'

At last Spring has sprung! The grey winter skies have been replaced by a soft blue. Fluffy white clouds hover and the first rays of the Spring-time sun peek out from behind them. There is a sense of optimism as the migrating birds return home once more. The sound of bird -calls fills the air, and everything seems to come alive once more. To me Spring -time *is* love in action.

I was greeted this day by the ascended Master El Morya who wished to discuss this subject.

'Greetings once again, this is your friend El Morya. I would like to talk to you this day about my favourite subject – Love in action.

To do so I shall have to discuss with you a matter that some of you may feel to be a little challenging. Well, it is good to have your belief system challenged once in a while for it pushes you through your comfort zone and into unknown territory. Although this in itself is a false statement for indeed there are no "unknown territories" for all is known by God, for all is of God. The reason why it is good to move outside of your comfort zone every once in a while is because if you stay with what you know you will become stagnant.

'And so it is my task to ensure that you think and ponder on what I teach you, that you allow yourself, through my words, to be led out of this comfort zone.

'It is noted that there are some who are sending out energy to help heal the planet. I say to you that many of you are sending out energy because of guilt. Your underlying feelings are of guilt, guilt that you may collectively have 'ruined' the planet. I ask you this: What energy do you think is attached to guilt? The answer is fear. This is the emotion that is attached to guilt. So would you not say then that you are sending out fear? I urge you to consider this for there is enough fear in your world without adding to it.

'Now, I have another question for you to consider: What is the difference between compassion and love?

Compassion allows

Love changes.

'Think about this, for if you truly had compassion for your world you would allow. To have compassion moves you into love and it is only through love that you can heal and change situations.

'To be a Master requires that you only do that which is your truth, not everyone else's truth. If it is your truth to do planetary healing meditations and ceremonies you will know it, you will be very clearly guided and directed. If not, then do not be as a sheep, just following the herd because it makes life easier. Stay in your truth, even if it means walking alone.

'You cannot send out love when you have very little for yourself, it is like being the wounded healer. The way to have self - love is through compassion: Allow yourself to be just who you are. You see, many of you have a great deal of anger and hurt stored within, you cannot force yourselves to be loving. You would be best advised to acknowledge this anger and pain and then begin to dissolve it. The way to dissolve it is through compassion. Just say to yourself 'I acknowledge that I feel anger this day, but it's ok that I feel this way'. Speak gently to yourself, keep telling yourself that it is alright to feel this way, this is having compassion for yourself.

The more you allow through compassion the more love will start to come forth. Love changes energy and so it will dissolve the anger.

'Many still assume that they need to do something, either physically or through meditation and sending energy out. I wish you to know this - the biggest impact you can have in your world is to become a presence of healing. Heal yourselves first, then allow your words to heal, your touch to heal and your presence to heal. When you have become this presence everyone who comes into contact with you will begin to heal. Remember the Master Jesus was a presence for healing, he could heal just by being. People would be near him or just touch his clothing and be healed. You too can be this powerful a presence but you have first to acknowledge that it is your presence, your energy that heals, not what you do or send out. If you were a Light in this world why would you need to send out? You wouldn't. You would understand that all that was needed was just to be the Light. By being this healing presence you would be like a beacon of Light – this is what will change your world - not by sending energy out, but by pulling in, pull in Light through compassion.

'Now remember this. If you truly wish to be of service to your planet, you have to start within, we keep returning to this truth, - start within.. When you have compassion and love for yourselves

this love will mirror out into your world. Truly this is the only way you will change your world, you will never heal her, others or yourself through guilt - have compassion and allow. Do not be under the false impression that you have to try and heal everyone that comes to you with a sad tale to tell. If you have compassion for these people then you will allow them their journey.'

I said to El Morya: "But I suppose we feel helpless, and that we should be doing something to put things right. Does that also mean that we should never heal anyone then? That doesn't feel very compassionate?"

'What I am saying is to learn to recognise when to offer assistance and when not to, go to your truth. Do not be a martyr, feeling that it is your duty to help everyone. If someone comes to you heavily burdened with troubles, check that it is right for you to help them first. If it is not right for you to do anything, then, as a compassionate being, trust this and just allow them their journey. Their Soul may have decided that it was time for them to begin their healing process. Sometimes it can be painful to begin a healing process, particularly if there is a lot to turn around and look at. If you try to assist them, save them from their pain, you could

be doing more harm than good for you might be interfering with their process. The greatest love you can have for another is to allow them their journey. We have to allow you your journey, to learn and grow through your experiences. To step in and try and save you from having painful experiences would be interfering with your free will.

'Do not allow guilt to get in the way of living your truth. To live your truth requires that you ask yourself if you want or feel it is right for you to do something. If you feel it is not right then you need to ask yourself 'Why not?' In other words, always check your motives in case there is fear that is trying to sabotage you. However, if you have checked your motives and it is simply not your truth , do not do it. Do not do something out of guilt – this is fear. Live your truth. If you ignore your truth, doing something when you do not want to, you will do it with resentment. It is therefore important to check your truth – follow it, for then resentment cannot reside within you.'

I asked: "How do we then make sure it is our truth we are following?"

'Well, as I mentioned, check your motives, and your feelings – if it feels right then do it. Learn to enhance your psychic abilities, your senses.'

I asked: "How?"

'To enhance your psychic abilities you have first to learn to follow them! Follow the signs given around you through life. The more you follow your "hunches" the more these abilities will develop. However, signs are not necessarily given like lightening - bolts form the sky, they are subtle. They could be as subtle as animals that cross your path, an impulse to read a book, a piece of music that you will hear, a message on some advertisement board. Most of humanity live their lives so unconscious that they miss these signs, and therefore do not receive their guidance.

'Now there is another thing I wish to discuss, and that is that once you have received your guidance – via these hunches and subtle messages, it is important to follow them! Stop the continual asking of what the outcome may be - it matters not the outcome. There is no need always to know the outcome of every situation – just let the journey unravel. We understand that when situations in your life are difficult and it is a struggle for you to calm your fears,

you desire to know the outcome. Perhaps to help you put it into perspective and thus view it from a larger picture, try to remember that it is just a chapter in your life – it's just a chapter – that's all it is. Now it is important with any 'chapter' that you contemplate what the chapter is trying to teach you about yourself. What is it that needs mastering? Go within and look at it.'

I asked him what did 'go within' really mean. I had heard it mentioned many times before but was still unsure what it really meant.

'To go within means contemplation – to contemplate self. When you contemplate self and you gain an understanding you become 'in light of Self'. To be 'in Light of' something means to have an understanding. This is self awareness. The more self aware you become the more enlightened you become. Enlightenment is therefore a gradual process. The more you go within, contemplate self, become self aware and gain an understanding the more awareness you will have. You will eventually reach a point where you are so self aware that the balance finally tips and enlightenment is reached.

'So contemplate yourself often, contemplate yourself through others and life around you, see yourself in all things – as a mirror.

'Let us return to the topic of compassion and love. I mentioned that you cannot truly love outside of self if you do not first love from within. Now, if you have stored emotions, issues that need looking at, why not go on a boredom retreat! Many ones, as we have already discussed in this book, seek entertainment so as to avoid facing self. I would recommend a boredom retreat often! Go somewhere where you are alone for at least one day and one night. Turn off music, TV. and other outside distractions, just sit. Do not read or find something to take your mind off of self - contemplate self. Now you will find that when you become bored many emotions will surface, just allow them to come up. Take yourself right into being bored – I know it sounds boring! But it is a good method to release these buried emotions. You will experience emotions that you never even knew were there. It may not be what you might consider to be fun, but it is designed to bring you a little closer to self. It is in the stillness that you will find yourself. Masters do not experience boredom, for we have looked at all parts of ourselves and learnt from them. We are content and peaceful within and so boredom is something we do not experience any longer. You too will experience this, but only if you stop running.'

'Now, remember this, everyone is trying to change the world from outside of themselves. If there is conflict in your reality then there is conflict within you. If there was no conflict within then there would be no conflict outside. Everyone wants to have a deep sense of inner peace in their lives. You cannot have peace when there is conflict within. Likewise peace cannot be gained outside of self. To move somewhere else, find a different job, to change a partner or to win a million pounds is not going to give you the peace you are looking for. You may feel better for a while, but it shall be short lived, it is not lasting. It is not lasting because it is outside of self. Where there is conflict there cannot be peace. The proper order is to first allow in the way that I have already mentioned. When you allow there is compassion, love follows, for compassion and love work hand in hand. Where there is true compassion there shall be true love. Where there is true love there shall be compassion, you cannot have one without the other. This is loving without conditions. And so there is a natural flow that takes place: Compassion>Love>Peace. Peace shall not live where there is conflict. If you want a better world then sort out yourselves first.

'For most of you it would take too long to go deeply into each issue within you. To look and understand all of your insecurities, all of your fears, all of your resentments. You would have to return again and again to do so. Many attend lengthy courses and workshops to try and 'empty their cupboards' and free their pasts. You do not have time for all of this processing, nor is there a need to do so. This creates conflict within, it is trying to 'rid yourselves' from something that you dislike about yourselves. Forget these long lengthy and often expensive methods, try having compassion instead! Acknowledge that you feel a certain way and tell yourself it is ok. You shall gain peace and harmony and shall stop swinging to and fro emotionally. You wonder why we do not step in and help you more in life, it is because we have compassion, we allow you your journey.'

"I would like to ask about enlightenment and if it is something only for Light Beings?"

'Good question. The answer, however, may surprise you a little, for the answer is No. If you re- read what I have just taught you about enlightenment, it is gained through self awareness is it

not? To be self aware does not necessarily mean that you are a 'good guy'. To put this into language that you understand, a repetitive murderer, for example can contemplate 'himself' and his actions, he too can become self aware. He can become enlightened then through his own experience. Now interestingly someone like this would probably have very little fear and probably very little guilt. These are the two things that many on the quest of becoming in-light-of-Light – would have the most difficulty releasing. And so a 'dark' person can become 'in light of' dark – so to speak.'

I questioned this for although I found it interesting, I also found it a little alarming, "Are you saying that a murderer doesn't need to 'lighten up' in order to be a Master?"

'This is exactly what I am saying! There are plenty of Lords of Darkness - and yes they are evolved beings! You do not necessarily need to evolve through Light – this would be limiting.'

"So how do they grow?" I asked.

'Through their own experience. You do not need only Light experiences to grow and evolve.'

I was persistent: "But surely there has to come a point where they would have to let go of their darkness in order to merge back into the oneness of God?"

'No, not let go of – integrate is a better description. Now, if a Master was a Master of darkness he would know himself very well in that darkness but he would not know himself in his Lightness. Therefore to become 'whole' he would need to integrate his Lightness. Now don't you think this is rather interesting, given that many are trying to know themselves through Light and Light only? Do you not see that this is not wholeness either?

'And so as we have said many times before, do not hide away your darkness – embrace it!

'If it is your choice to gain wholeness then have compassion for your dark side. To look with compassion at your darkness (perhaps on your boredom retreat) will soften your dark edges. Remember – where there is compassion – love follows. It is love that changes energy.

'This then is Love – In – Action.'

CHAPTER 8

LORDS OF DARKNESS

'There are more ways to evolve than just through Light!'

El Morya, I discovered, is one of those Masters who likes to push you out of your comfort zone with a size ten boot! He is not for the faint-hearted amongst us, nor is he for those who like the softly softly approach. He has always been very direct and to the point and I didn't expect him to be any different in this chapter.

I called upon him so that I could ask him some more questions about these Dark Lords that he had mentioned in the previous chapter. It was about a week later when he showed up. I have learnt that the Masters come in their own time, and so quite often I would be left for a few days to ponder about what they had taught me. They would show up when they were ready, not when I, in my impatience wanted them.

'Good evening, yes I have returned to enlighten you a little more. Now, I explained that these Dark Lords grow through their own experience did I not? Well, here is what I want you to learn. God, your creator, loves all of his creation. He is not selective. It is hard for you to imagine the greatness of God's love for His creation. So great is His love that He allows you to express yourselves as you wish. He does not interfere for He is the observer.

'Now, you yourself have understood that your dark moments, the darkest points in your life, have led you to a deeper understanding about yourself. In other words, you have grown from the experience. You may not wish to experience some things again, and that is not necessary. What is necessary is that you gain some understanding from the experience.'

"OK, so we learn from our experiences. If we then contemplate self we become self aware. You mentioned that to learn through Light and Light only is limiting. Can you tell me more?"

'Yes. Well, it's as we mentioned in the very first chapter, to stay in a "Light room" is a trap. Many in the New Age movement are in this room. To live in this room is limiting. This Light room is

spirituality that is ungrounded. It is knowledge without demonstration. It is one thing to know about transcending pain, illness, poverty, to be able to biolocate etc, but another to demonstrate it. To demonstrate means to let go of fear first, to let go of fear means to face it – head on. To face it means to come out of that Light room.'

"Can you explain about the life of a Dark Lord once he/she has moved beyond this dimension?"

'Well their life would be whatever they created it to be. They, as you, are not limited in their expression.

'Now, let me back track slightly here. Let me guide you back to the point before they left the Earth plane. Understand that a Lord of Darkness would leave the Earth plane and the third dimension the same as everyone else. They travel through the same vortex – the same tunnel of Light that would carry them into the new dimension. Now here is where it may get a little challenging, and you will need to have an open mind and heart to accept this.

The higher dimensions are not solely for those of Light.

There are not places for Dark and places for Light beings solely.

'The fifth dimension, for example, is not just reserved for the Light, if this were so, where do you think your dark brothers and sisters would go? Which dimension? Taking into account that there is no such place as Hell this poses somewhat of a dichotomy wouldn't you say?

'And so the Dark move through the same tunnel of Light and are helped across just the same as any being. They would eventually go through their life review and re-live their lives exactly as you will. Whether they return or evolve onwards depends on many factors. Let us suppose that this Soul would not return to Earth. He/she would then go to a dimension with a vibration that matched. Now you may think that someone who was a murderer, for example, would move to a very low vibrational dimension, but this is not necessarily so. At this point I wish to remind you not to judge these Souls. We have seen you all shaking your heads in disbelief that someone could kill another. Well, let me remind you, that throughout all of your incarnations you have all been the murderer! Yes, you have all taken another's life for some reason. Now, taking this into account, I ask you this: did you go to Hell? Do you at this point in your incarnation cycle, feel as if you had been cast into the fires that burn in Hell? If so, did someone then take pity on you and let you have another try on Earth? Or perhaps you

suffered long enough at the hands of Demons and repented, confessed at being an Evil person! (and to think that you all thought that you were Lightworkers, you must of had a 180 degree turn around!) OK, so who was it then that decided you should go to Hell? And who decided that you had suffered enough in Hell to be allowed out again? Take a quick look at your body, are there scars from this raging fire? Of course there are not, because you never went into one, and nor shall these Souls.

'What I want you to understand is that there is not segregation. There are not quarantine restrictions in the Universe nor are there sign-posts reading "Dark, keep out!". This is a fantasy created by your religions. It also has served you to believe this because you feel safer to think that you might be out of harm's way, so to speak.

'Let's take a look at the life of Adolph Hitler. Adolph was a man on the Earth that is considered to be Evil. Now I hesitate a little about mentioning this 'great' man because many focus on him and yet there are many, many others just as great in their darkness.

'I can see that you are a little shocked at my choice of words, particularly one – 'great'. Well, be shocked1 It is good for you, for it gets you thinking. Now, I chose the word 'great' because that is what he was, and still is. You do not need to be only great in Light, the Darkness can be great also - and is. Understand that the

greatness of the dark is very powerful. Now I am telling you this because you need to know the greatness of God in ALL of His creation. And so, Adolph evolved through his darkness. He contemplated his power and became self aware, he became in Light of his Darkness.'

I asked about people who abuse children. "How does it affect them on a Soul level and also how does it affect the children, the innocents, on a Soul level?"

'The Soul understands it is Spirit, travelling through time and space experiencing, and so on a Soul level it is detached. It is on the personality level that it is shocked and traumatised. Therefore the abuser would have to be judged by God if there was a form of punishment. There isn't. Now, there are many reasons why a Soul on a higher level would chose to come back and be abused. For some they had been the abuser that had had his/her life review, contemplated and decided to experience life from the other view-point. Sometimes they choose to help open a number of people's heart chakras through the immense feelings of love that can be stirred up through these experiences. This is quite a common choice. It is done out of service to others who have had difficulty

opening their heart chakras. They have needed a "shock" to push the energy up enough to open them. Now when this is the role of the child you usually find that these are the ones that leave through the abuse. In other words were murdered by the abuser. They had done what they came to do and left. The purpose was to open others' heart chakras, it was not meant to send others into rage and feelings of hate for the murderer.

Here we are given the challenge of forgiveness.

'If you truly had compassion for these children you would have respect for what they had came to do and would honour their life by forgiving and letting go. If this can be achieved then the child's mission would have not been in vain.'

I expressed that this seemed a little cold, almost as if we are to be without any feelings.

'Well I can tell you that your world would be a much better place if you didn't have such strong feelings! It is usually these strong feelings that result in murder in the first place.

'But to answer your question. You are looking at it from a third dimensional perspective, where you see life and death, good and bad – polarity. From a higher dimension we understand that there

is no end to life, you are eternal! In truth there cannot be a end to a life, it is just progression.

'You feel that I am being cold and emotionless, and yet if I had strong emotions I would never have ascended – I Mastered my emotions. The strong emotions that you speak of come out of fear – I have none. You are outraged when you hear of a murder or some form of abuse because it stirs up fear within you. Perhaps you fear for your own children or even your own life. You feel sadness for the families concerned. I understand why you accuse me of being cold-hearted when I am so detached about such matters, and yet in truth we consider you all to be our family. You are all our family, one big one, and we weep with compassion when you do. However, as I mentioned in the previous chapter, we allow you your journey. You have to allow Souls their journey, no matter what their journey brings. Therefore I am not asking you to become cold- hearted, indeed not. I am asking you to have compassion for all those concerned, and this is very different.'

"OK, I shall try. I wonder if you can tell me what the role of the Dark Lords is?"

'Well there is no role as such, only expansion. To have a specific role would be limiting'.

Now I was confused! "I thought that they were meant to hold the balance for the polarity that is here in our third dimension?"

'No. You manage that very well yourselves! Understand that you all carry within you the 'Devil and the Christ'. You already hold the polarity in place. You do not need anyone to do it for you. It is when the two can be married, can come peacefully together, that you then move out of polarity and out of a polarity dimension.

'Now, I just wish to back track slightly so as to clear up some confusion before it occurs.

'I mentioned that the Dark Lords – or indeed anyone – do not have specific roles and missions and that it was just expansion, Souls experience life. Now having said this I wish to mention that that there are some advanced Souls who sometimes chose to return to teach something specific. Hence the abused children that I have just talked about. These are advanced Souls, the less advanced amongst you are not on any special mission, you are just trying to remember who you are! This seems to keep many of you busy throughout life-time after life-time! When I say remember who you

are, I of course mean that you are trying to remember that you are God creating in human form. You forgot this, and seem to think that you are Humans trying to become God, or worse still that you are Humans who have to worship other gods, and this is not so.'

I was curious if the Light and the Dark Lords lived side by side. This seemed very unlikely, but I put this question to El Morya.

'If they so desired, then yes. As I have said there is no restriction as such. However, I wish for you to remember this Universal rule: Like attracts like. Therefore Souls draw to them beings of the same vibration. And so this is where you get your Hell theory from. In other words, Dark Lords would draw to them other beings through their vibration and through their experiences.

'For example, is it not fair to say that on Earth people who have certain interests seem to find that they attract people to them who have the same interests? Now isn't that strange! Well, not so strange, you attract them to you by your vibration. Your interests hold a vibration and so others who have the same interests draw close to you, you are all like large magnets! And so, the same applies in other realms. Those who have had certain experiences

will find that those around them also had similar experiences. I wish for you to know that this does not mean that you will all end up in one large room together. It is very likely that you will never meet up with a Dark Lord on another level, they would have very little interest in you. Note my wording – Interest. In other words, you do not share the same interests or experiences, and so your vibration would not be compatible.'

"I would like to ask about negative ET's and about abductions. Are these also the Dark Lords?"

'No not necessarily. You see a Dark Lord is a being who is consciously Dark, they are Masters of Darkness. A being from another world – or ET's as you call them - live by different rules. Some of them have had emotions bred out of them and so do not understand your human emotions. They would be confused as to why you get emotional about "sharing information" – or what you call abducted.'

"Well it's because it's against our free will."

'But they do not understand free will, it is not something they experience in their world and so they have no knowledge of it. These beings would not be considered to be Dark Lords. They find you curious, and wish to learn from your emotions, they are not "Evil". Many have watched you evolve through your emotions and now wish to experience for themselves emotions so that they too may advance. And so some of you have been abducted so that you could be mated with. This is to reintroduce emotions within their DNA.'

I mentioned that I thought a lot of people might find this information a little frightening.

'That is because a lot of people have a lot of fear! You could always chose to view it as service. You are aiding other civilisations and species to evolve and grow.'

I wondered if this still takes place, as we seem to hear less about abductions these days.

'No, it does not happen so much these times, for the seed has been sown. The emotions have been planted within their DNA and so there is not the need to merge with more of you.'

"You mentioned that Dark Lords are conscious of their darkness, but are there any Dark Lords that are ET's?"

'Of course. And as I've already explained, it is their choice to experience life in this way.'

"Are there wars between the Dark Lords and the Light Lords?"

'There are indeed wars that take place and have done so since the "beginning of time." (I wish to remind you here that there is no beginning as there is no end). However, many times throughout Earth's history beings have tried to dominate and take control of this little planet. Likewise there are wars in other realms and on other planets.'

"And does the Light always prevail?"

'I think you have been watching too many Star Trek movies! It is not about who wins and who loses, that would be competition, and we are uninterested in competition. To put it very simply, the Light are the peacemakers and the Dark are the lawbreakers, they like to be disruptive.'

"Does this disruption take place in the higher dimensions as well, or is it just for the lower realms?"

'Any realm. Even in the Angelic realms. It can be quite lively you know, they do not sit around on white fluffy clouds playing harps all day! It can be disruptive on any level until one becomes pure Light. It is at that level when one moves out of any form and exists in pure Light. You would be considered to be very advanced to reach this level. Any being who were to enter into this would be transformed into Light. And so you would not expect a Dark Lord to enter into this realm because he/she would not feel comfortable approaching it. Remember, there is no judgement, it would not be "out of bounds" for them, but they would feel uncomfortable. The love that is Light would in a sense be too strong.'

"So can you tell me the procedure they would have to go through in order to enter into this Light realm?"

'You tell me! You are the ones experiencing this! There are a lot of fears and dark areas that you are all working on. There are parts of your beingness that you do not love. It is only when you love all that you are, love others equally and indeed all of life – even those scary Dark brothers and sisters – that you become pure love, pure love means without conditions. When you are pure love you vibrate at a very high frequency. When this frequency matches that realm of pure Light you shall enter into it and not before. In other words you can only go where your vibration matches. Again, I come back to that Universal law – "Like attracts like." When you have learned to love all parts of self you move beyond fear, after all, what would there then be to fear? To have pure love is to be fearless.'

CHAPTER 9

ASCENSION

'The only difference between you and us is the vibration.'

When I first heard the word Ascension it triggered me in some profound way. It was as if an alarm bell rang inside of me. When I say alarm bell, it was more of a 'wake–up' call. That wake-up call left a sense of anticipation and excitement, even though I didn't really understand what it was!

This was during the 1990's, and there were some wonderful channelled tapes by Eric Klein going around at that time, talking about Ascension as being more of an evacuation. This evacuation was to lift us onto space craft whilst the Earth went through her magnificent changes. Well, looking back at it now I have to laugh at myself, for I was ready! My attitude was, 'When are we going!' I left notes around the house for friends and family explaining why I wasn't around and not to worry, I was safe in a space ship! I have to say that I am by no means criticising these tapes. Some of the information is now outdated but the energy that comes from them is still beautiful and potent.

When I mentioned Ascension to some of my friends, they told me that all Ascension meant was to Ascend in consciousness. I didn't feel comfortable with this - I was sure that there must be more to it. And so I asked my Ascended friends - after all, they should know!

'Ascending in consciousness is not the only option. There is mastery of the physical body also, to such a degree that Light enters into every cell of the physical body – not just the emotional and mental – and literally turns every cell into Light, leading finally to ascension of the physical body.

'Ascension of the physical body, therefore, means taking the physical body with you into eternity. These are just 'choices' , and one way is no better than the other. Whatever choice is right for you, Ascension means mastery of the physical plane so much so that the repeating pattern of 'reincarnation' into this plane ceases. In other words you 'outgrow' the third dimension. You can choose to ascend in consciousness, ascending all of the etheric bodies, leaving the physical one to go through the death process, or choose

mastery of the physical body, transforming it into Light and taking the physical body with you into other planes of existence. This then means that you choose not to experience the death process, it also means that you can come and go as you please, leave the Earth plane and returning at another time frame if you choose.'

I was told that Babaji and Thoth chose this method. Through the ascension process we transform our physical body into Light, and from that point on our focus and vehicle of consciousness becomes our Light Body. This does not age, and cannot become ill or die.

'Neither way is better and shouldn't be judged, it is just like choosing to travel by bus, car, bicycle or walk to get to a destination, you just choose a mode of transport, a vehicle to get you there.'

In a sense, leaving the physical body behind, to go through the death process is an easier option for most of us, for it involves less belief structures being broken down, and so we find it easier to understand.

Many of the Ascended Masters who have gone before us chose this option, creating a new vehicle of Light as they go through this process. This choice involves mastering the emotions to such a high level that the whole consciousness is raised. This is what many of us are in the process of doing right now.

When I think back to the time when I first started to work consciously with the Ascended Masters, I was absolutely certain that I would ascend physically. There was no doubt in my mind that I wouldn't. I couldn't understand why others laughed at me when I told them. I was told by so many people that, 'That is for the Masters – not us!' that I started to believe them. I put aside my belief in my own physical ascension and decided that yes, I wasn't 'evolved enough' to do that. And so I let it go.

Well, I continued to raise my consciousness for a few years, but somehow still felt that there was more to this process, should I choose it. It was only after my near death experience, some time later, that I regained my belief. I felt like a hypocrite, for we are taught to love the physical body – because it is our sacred temple and should be honoured. Why then should I wish to let it die and decay in the earth? It just didn't feel right to me. The Masters asked me:

'Do you love your body enough to take it with you? Do you honour it enough NOT to leave it behind?'

Then when I was lying in the bath one day, my inner voice asked which choice I was going to make. I said that I would really love to ascend and take my physical body with me, but surely I wasn't evolved enough for that to happen. The reply came that it is not such a big deal as I was making it out to be, and that it was nothing to do with being highly evolved. At this point in human evolution when the vibration of the whole planet is rising rapidly, it is simply a choice open to all. I asked 'How do I go about it then?' The reply came, *'Just request it, and then believe it will happen, not just a little bit, but really believe it -for thought creates. Re-programme your mind not to believe in the death process. Do not give in to old age, believe in youthfulness and eternal life – this is how!'*

I wanted to know more and so the Masters guided me to a set of teachings to study. This study was a real 'eye opener' in many ways! Through it I learned all about the different glands in the body, the cells and the brain. I learnt that we truly are God, for the presence of God is everywhere and within us all. Knowing this, we have to ask ourselves a question : 'How powerful do we believe God to be?' We could answer 'All-powerful' and so the second question has to be, 'Is there anything that God cannot do?' I don't believe so, so knowing that I have to ask myself, 'So, if God can do anything, and I have God flowing through me, is there anything that I cannot do?' The answer has to be No! So then we get to the point where we know that we can do anything - we simply just have to believe it.

I learnt that we are using very little of our brain, and that to open up all of our abilities and to open ourselves to receive 'super consciousness' requires us to operate on full brain capacity. Well then, how do we awaken our sleeping dormant brain? Through the will.

The pituitary gland is the master gland that sits in - between the left and right parts of the brain. It is the gland that, once fully active will awaken the rest of the brain. It will release hormones around the body and through this process our vibration rises, we eventually become a 'Christed being'. This, I learned, is all done by desiring it to be fully open, focusing and willing it.

Now, returning to the subject of physical Ascension, how does that happen? Every cell begins to vibrate at such a fast rate that it turns into Light. When this begins the temperature of the body increases and the body starts to glow with Light. When every cell is vibrating at a very high rate, you will disappear from normal vision and move into a higher dimensional reality. This is because the body has moved in vibration beyond the third dimension and is now vibrating on a much higher dimensional level. This then means that you will not go through the death process as you will then have a Light Body, the Biblical 'Garment of Light'. Ageing will not exist for you, and you will have stepped into the next dimensional reality. Simple isn't it! It just takes belief in ourselves, distancing ourselves – emotionally, not physically – from any belief pattern related to death, loving ourselves and God, and raising our vibration level. When we have *become* Light, we can step into the Light, and then access the next stage of our spiritual evolution.

At this point in my life I was working part-time in a residential home, caring for the elderly!. As you can imagine, it took great control on my part to stick to my beliefs whilst being surrounded by others who firmly believe in the death process and old age! I honour and respect their choice, but also feel that perhaps they didn't realise that there *was* a choice.

So again, how do we do it? By simply focusing our attention on the body and willing it to increase in vibration, and by being willing to remove every obstacle that prevents us from becoming Light. And in a way, this is an entirely natural process for us. We essentially ARE Light, and it was from Light that we came. By raising our vibration we simply enter fully into what we really are.

Whatever choice you make for yourself requires a certain degree of self mastery. In many ways it requires us to do a U-turn with our thoughts and attitudes. If we are to *become* the Master of our reality we must *be* the Master of our reality! Self mastery need not mean achieving great and extraordinary things, it is simply mastering our own limitations – whatever they may be. This is relative, for one man's fear limit is totally different from another's. For example, facing an angry army may be just as fearful for one as facing a small group of people and giving a speech is for another. It is all relative, and depends upon the size of your comfort zone and the levels of your fear. Therefore, there are no 'set tests' as such, and all levels of self mastery are very individual. To master self in the third dimension involves mastery of the physical, emotional and mental bodies. This depends on how much you have to clear and how difficult that may be.

Mastery of the physical body involves mastering habits, security, sexuality, food , drink, etc, all things associated with the first three chakras. Remember that all is relative to each individual. Habit-breaking therefore could be as small as simply stopping nail-biting. It could be to stop smoking, or it could be to stop taking drugs. Being able to let go of money can be extremely difficult for one person, whilst for another it may be easy. This depends on how attached you are. To master sexuality, without wishing to sound chauvinistic, may be harder for men! From my understanding it is not to abstain totally, for I believe in 'all things in moderation', but to raise it to the level of a much more loving experience. It is to master fantasies and the *need* for sex. For the mastering of food and drink, I would again say 'all things in moderation'. Food and drink should not be addictive, and they should be used as a way of sustaining our bodies until we reach the point where perhaps we choose not to partake in it any longer.

Mastery of the emotional body involves coming to terms with yourself, your life, your past and then letting go of it all. Becoming the observer rather than being lost in the drama. Letting go of self means letting go of an identity – this can feel a little scary when it happens, for you can feel lost and unsure about who you are. This is simply because we hide behind our identity and use it to give us confidence. To let go of your life means letting go of those things in life that you have outgrown, become safe and comfortable with, but no longer serve you. It is about having self-control and not indulging in emotional outbursts. Working through grief, anger, fear, jealousy, hatred, and learning to exercise forgiveness is all part of this.

Mastery of the mental body requires that you learn to live consciously. It involves being aware of your thoughts and your words, to such a degree that you are creating positive and uplifting experiences for yourself in life. Having thoughts and using words that raise your consciousness instead of lowering it. Speaking the truth at all times - never lying is part of being a Master.

I was in the bath (again!) and was thinking about my cells as being conscious and therefore having a consciousness. And so I decided on an experiment I asked my cells what would help to raise my vibration, and turn my body into Light, transforming any dense matter into Light.

I had quite an interesting conversation with my cells. I think it may be helpful to share this with you. This is what my cells said:

'Stop watching films that involve violence or density of any form, for the vibration coming from the film/programme is killing the Light within you. Also stop watching the news'.

I asked why, for I liked to be informed about what is going on around the world.

'If you increase your vibration, becoming one with All of life, you will know what is going on, for you will have become it. You will then have the truth rather than a very limited view from your news which is based on fear'.

By now I was out of the bath and putting cream on my face!

'Why are you putting that on?'

'Because it's part of my self-love procedure!' I answered.

'Can you not love yourself without manufactured creams? In a sense you are programmed to buy all of these things in order to love self.'

'Well, also to look youthful and healthy.'

'Are you saying that to look old is to look unhealthy then? Do you not see you have fallen into mass consciousness again that says if you look old you are unhealthy which in turn is what causes death. If a young person were to die you would assume they had been ill –unhealthy, because young people don't die – only old people do!'

'Well, it's nice to look youthful.'

'Why do you want to? What is your motivation for youthing? To become God you must let go of image to such a degree that it does not matter if you look old, wrinkled, fat, thin. Only then shall you know God fully. The vibration of all cells shall raise to encompass Light so much that you shall glow. When this happens you look very soft and beautiful no matter what the age. This is not to say that there is anything wrong in looking and feeling youthful, quite the reverse, for it should be natural to do so. However, it is the motive that lies behind your desire that needs looking at.'

I then asked about foods, and if there are any I shouldn't eat in order to help raise my vibration.

'Eat and drink whatever you like, it is only your thoughts about the foods that have the effect, not the foods themselves.'

I then asked about Masters and Angels and about the process of communicating with them, and if it's a case of just continually raising your vibration.

'The only difference between you and them is the vibration. Humanity lives most of its time in low vibrational thoughts. If it were to lift its thoughts and hold them at a high level continuously then yes, everyone would commune with the Angels. The only reason why humans are not in continuous communication with these beings is because angelic consciousness is held in a high frequency band. They do not enter into dense, low wave band thought patterns. Every time you have a thought or say a word, a coloured wave band is sent out from you. How 'uplifting' the thought or word was, determines how far it travels up in the vibrational levels. Someone who is full of fear and density and thinks and speaks only in these terms would not reach a very high

vibrational level. This is why it is so important to master your thoughts and words, for if you want to be a Master then you have to start thinking like one! So understand this, you cannot be a Master if you have not mastered your thoughts and your words.'

I wanted to ask about my work. At the time I was working as I already mentioned, as a carer for the elderly people in a dementia unit. I asked how I could stop the work from making me feel tired and worn out.

'Well, you have lost your joy for the work. Joy is energising. Unhappiness is tiring'

"Well, when I have days off, I feel tired - not unhappy, just tired what causes that?"

'Then you would be processing and releasing a former thought form of unhappiness.'

"So are you then saying that when you are tired and exhausted it is always because of processing unhappiness?"

'Yes, happiness is Light, and this is never tiring, only uplifting.'

"Well suppose you have a really happy day and laugh a lot, but still feel very tired at the end of the day?"

'The happiness would have loosened a stored memory, nostalgia, a fond memory which brings with it a touch of sadness as well as fondness. This nostalgia is dragging up the past, and that pursuit is very tiring'.

"So you're saying that reminiscing is tiring?"

'Yes, whether it brings a good or a bad memory it's still carrying past baggage. Baggage is very tiring and exhausting.'

"So if I let go of all baggage I will not feel over-tired or exhausted again?"

'Yes, as long as you also remain true to yourself. Let go of baggage and be true to self at all times. To be true to self at all times means not doing things to please others, always follow your heart, and never lie.'

Finally then, the Masters tell us that we are equal to them, but I do not believe that many of us on the Earth feel like that, especially when we are going through clearing things!

'You are all equal, just at different levels of growth. It is like a flower - most of humanity is like a bud just opening. The Masters therefore are in full bloom, revealing their true beauty. But the flower is also beautiful when closed - it is still the same flower, just at a different stage of evolution.'

CHAPTER 10

A NEW WORLD

'You are the peace makers, you have set firm foundations, it is for the next generation to instigate it.'

And so finally, a word about these times. As we know and feel, there is a quickening occurring. We feel it within us - everything seems to be speeding up, and the best advice from the Masters is to try and slow down! There is a great deal of fear within people, and for those still 'asleep' it is an extremely fearful time. For those of us awake it seems a challenge to hold it all together amongst all the chaos. The Masters have warned me for some time that we have had all of the training and preparation that we need to get us through these times. We would have been wise to have worked on ourselves, clearing density and our past to enable us to move forward into the new world with ease. We all know how the Masters can heal themselves, create their realities consciously, transport themselves into different dimensions and go beyond the usual human accomplishments. The question has to be – can we? In other words it is no use just knowing about these abilities, we have to learn to master them. When I asked El Morya to explain about becoming a Master he had this to say:

'When you thought that I was being strict with you, and I told you I was being focused, I told you this for a reason. To be focused at all times is the key to becoming a Master. You have to master your words and your thoughts. As we have mentioned, every word that you say and every thought that you think creates your reality. Every time you use the word I – then that is how you will be. You all know of this, and yet still you continue to be 'helpless' victims of your circumstances. Many ones have had lots of affirmations pinned up around their houses. Every room you go in there is an affirmation about this or that. This is good in the sense that it helps to keep you focused, but then you sabotage yourselves immediately by your unconscious thoughts. You may well have good intentions when you do your meditations and affirmations but you seem to have difficulty in holding the focus throughout the day. For example it is no use meditating, creating and affirming that you are abundant and then throughout the day acting as though you

are poor. Do you not see that you have instantly self-sabotaged your creations and all the good work that you have done? You are being part-time Masters! If you truly want abundance then you have to live it, think it, feel it and be it.

'Many of you, we note, wish to be a Master, well you will never be one if you only work part time at it. To be a Master requires that you live throughout your day as one, not just when it suits you.! To become a Master requires you to live as one twenty four hours per day until you become one. So you will need to Master your thoughts, words, health, intentions and motives, Master all habits, emotions and fears. You need to Master yourself throughout your day – every day.

'Some of you seem to have the idea that Masters were born with special dispensations and so it was easier for them. Well for most that was untrue, the majority of Ascended Masters lived very 'normal' lives. They just had a strong will, and a desire to have control over their lives.

'And so you see there are no excuses as to why you too cannot Master your own lives and Ascend beyond this plane. All it takes is working at, something many ones find hard, for in some ways you are lazy. You start off with good intentions and then become bored and give up. You must learn to train yourselves to such a degree

that you create – exactly – the life that you would wish for yourselves. Learn to have unlimited thoughts. The more unlimited you are in your thoughts the more unlimited you shall become. So why not think to yourself thoughts such as "I am extraordinarily gifted, I am fabulously wealthy, I am destined to be a great Master on Earth." You see God doesn't limit you – you do.

'The more self- mastery – which incidentally is another word for self- control - that you have, the more Light enters into your bodies.

The more Light enters into your bodies, the higher your vibration becomes.

The higher your vibration becomes, the higher the vibration of the environment around you becomes. The higher the vibration of the environment around you becomes, the more you help the planet.

"This is the way it works, this is the way that all of the Masters have diligently worked throughout all of time. The more Light that you anchor within you the more resistance and density you release.

'Now you will often hear the term density, but what is it? Well density is that which is limiting – fears, baggage from the past. Sadness, lust, greed, gluttony, jealousy, etc. could all be called

density. Do you know what one of the biggest forms of density is in Man? His past. You just do not seem to be able to let go of it! Because of your past you keep going round and around in circles, recreating a treadmill type existence for yourselves. I can tell you that you can never be in the Now when you carry the past. Let go of it!

'Now, we have spoken about Light and about anchoring Light. This is occurring within you, and also around your planet. She is mirroring back the same process that you are going through. Hers often occurs in a much bigger way, for she has a bigger body, but it is still the same process.

'So, never fear change, whether it be within you or within the planet, for it is a beautiful sign that Light is coming in. Now when Light comes into the brain and the rest of the body, it doesn't always feel good! You can expect some headaches, light-headedness, dizziness, aching of muscles, and perhaps even a weight increase around the Hara. It is good not to be 'hung up' about your appearance! If this occurs it is nothing to be concerned about, for it is simply Light trying to ground you, stopping you from being too 'spacey'. Any of these symptoms are just a sign of Light throwing out density. All of these symptoms will decrease once the activation has been complete.'

I always found the Masters' words and energies to be very comforting. They told me that the more Light that we embrace within us, so too will others find us comforting to be around. It is therefore important that we have our boundaries. I asked the Masters to explain to me the process that we will go through and they said:

'*We don't know, it's never been done before in this way!*'

They assured me, however, that we shall be supported all the way through the process.

'You know that you are loved, not only by us – your brothers and sisters, but by the Ultimate Source of life – named God.

'I can tell you at this time that the magnetic fields of your planet are fluctuating energetically, and this affects you. It affects you in many ways. Some find it very difficult to focus, they become sleepy, and withdrawn, some are emotional, tearful or grumpy. Some may find it difficult to sleep if this is the case, it is wise to get up and try and sleep later on in the day if you need to.

'Throughout this time , and this is what is known as the 'null zone', life will seem very strange. There will be a peculiar stillness, for you are entering into the void. The void is nothing to fear. It is simply the means of moving through dimensions, it is very womb-like and nurturing. Try and focus on being held in a womb, rather than panicking, which will only send you straight into your emotional body – and this certainly will not help!

'Use this time now to practise your focus as we have taught you.

'You may well notice that many of you are feeling a pull to move – and quickly! For those of you who are already well rooted into your homes, you will be noticing by now a change in the energy around and within your homes. This energy change is due to an energy field that is being installed around your homes. This energy field holds you, almost like suspending you in a higher vibration, to aid you through the transition.

'We are unable to say how long this period will last, but when you emerge you will feel the change within your beingness. There will be a clarity, a clearness to the Light. Your eyesight will be sharper, and this is already occurring. Your senses - taste, touch, sight, and sound will be much sharper. A new way of living will emerge which is much more harmonious, humanity will work

together rather than separately. Countries will unite and help each other, and religious differences will come to an end. People will have more humility and sympathy for others and for wildlife. Animals and vegetation will be valued instead of exploited.

'You my dear friends, have been the peacemakers, you have set firm foundations for this to take place. It is for the next generation to instigate it, these children are the ones who will bring into fruition what you started.

'This is the time and you are the ones that have been prophesised - it will be the beginning of a new world! There will be much to celebrate, for to move through these times means to Go Beyond Fear.

'We love you dearly.

'So Be It.